ADVANCE PRAISE

"Scott MacKenzie has taken the complexity out of personal finance with a story you'll actually enjoy reading. *The Lobster League* shows you how real people make money mistakes—and how you can avoid them."

GREG CRABTREE
Author of *Simple Numbers, Straight Talk, Big Profits*

"Scott MacKenzie's *The Lobster League* provides readers with sound advice to navigate successful transitions not only with their financial capital but also in their lives. His fiduciary expertise rings through with confidence and clarity."

JAMES E. HUGHES JR., ESQ.
Author of *Family Wealth: Keeping it in the Family*

"I first heard Scott speak on behavioral finance at an Entrepreneurs' Organization event and was captivated by his storytelling. *The Lobster League* brings that same engaging style to the page, delivering powerful insights through a compelling narrative. What sets this book apart is how it imparts wisdom not by lecturing, but by immersing you in a story that makes the lessons stick with you. The result is an entertaining and enlightening read that will leave any entrepreneur wiser and inspired."

ETHAN KING
TEDx speaker, bestselling author of *Wealth Beyond Money* and *ChatGPT To Double Your Business In 90 Days*

THE LOBSTER LEAGUE

THE LOBSTER LEAGUE

A FABLE ABOUT PERSONAL FINANCE

Scott R. MacKenzie, MBA,
CFP®, CIMA®, CLU®
Senior Wealth Advisor, Managing Member, PFW Advisors

The Lobster League
A Fable About Personal Finance

Copyright © 2025 by Scott R. MacKenzie

Disclaimer: This book has been published for the purpose of providing the reader with general information on its subject matter. The author and the publisher believe the information to be accurate and authoritative at the time of publication. The book is sold with the understanding that neither the author nor the publisher is providing professional advice, and the reader should not rely upon this book as such. Every situation is different, and professional advice (whether psychological, legal, financial, tax, or otherwise) should only be obtained from a professional licensed in your jurisdiction who has knowledge of the specific facts and circumstances.

Cover Design by Louis and Kathy Kahill
Interior Layout and Design by Brittany Becker
Editorial Team: Ginny Glass, Jamie Smith, Kiska Carr

ISBNs:
E-book: 979-8-89165-355-9
Paperback: 979-8-89165-356-6
Hardcover: 979-8-89165-357-3

Published by:
Streamline
Kansas City, MO
shareyourstory.com

Streamline
BOOKS

"The most important quality for an investor
is temperament, not intellect."
—WARREN BUFFETT

"The biggest investing errors come not from
factors that are informational or analytical,
but from those that are psychological."
—HOWARD MARKS

"Investors are prone to overconfidence, to overreacting to
the market, and to misjudging probabilities. Understanding
these biases is essential to making sound financial decisions."
—DANIEL KAHNEMAN

"Behavioral finance does not tell us that people are
irrational. It tells us that people are predictably irrational."
—HERSH SHEFRIN

"We can't do without psychology, because
without it, economics is incomplete."
—RICHARD THALER

*To my family, who have always been my true wealth; to
the clients who entrusted me with their dreams; and to
future generations, may this book remind you that the
greatest return comes from living life deliberately.*

TABLE OF CONTENTS

Introduction. XI

1. Creating the Lobster League 1

2. The Overconfident Shipbuilder. 11

3. The Herding Farmers. 21

4. Harmony and Strength 35

5. Cold Cash 49

6. Old Dog, New Tricks 61

7. Golden Visions 73

8. A Team Sport 87

9. Lost at Sea 101

10. Mad Money 113

11. Transitions 127

12. Rational Finance 137

Note from the Author 147

INTRODUCTION

THANK YOU for taking a chance on *The Lobster League*. As a financial advisor, I've long wanted to share my experience with a wider audience so more people can make better, more informed financial decisions.

Why Write a Book—And Why a Fable?

Over the past thirty years, I've seen people fall into similar patterns with money. A common one? Jumping into investing. It's exciting, scary, or simply feels like the responsible thing to do. While those feelings are valid, they often get overtaken by human nature, blinding us to what truly creates a satisfying life.

The problem is that satisfaction is deeply personal. I've never met two people with the same definition. Yet many approach their financial goals using the same cookie-cutter strategies. That rarely works.

That's why I chose a fable. It's a way to introduce key concepts through relatable, readable stories. While the characters and events are fictional, the scenarios are familiar. Chances are, you'll recognize similar patterns in the lives of people around you—and eventually, in your own.

How Should You Use This Book?

Start by stepping back. Reflect on your decisions. Are you confident you're on the right path? If the answer is no, it may be time to reassess how you're making decisions. That kind of pause can be incredibly valuable. I do it myself, often.

Your time is limited—so don't waste it living someone else's life.
—STEVE JOBS

Chapter 1

CREATING THE LOBSTER LEAGUE

T HINK FAST!"

Alan Sanderson's two favorite words growing up occurred whenever his father, a former semipro hockey player in their native Gloucester, Massachusetts, would fire a puck at him on the frozen pond near their home during childhood winters, or a football with a tight spiral, or a fastball with zip during warmer months. Alan would have to react quickly to avoid being hit in the head by one of his father's fast-moving missiles. As a result, Alan became a decent athlete himself, playing college hockey at the nearby University of New Hampshire, although his NHL dreams would never be realized.

Instead, Alan developed a love of numbers and a desire for financial security, not just for himself but also for the working-class families from his hometown. Most people associate Gloucester with outsized wealth, gorgeous vacation cottages, and summers at the beach. While all of that is true, Gloucester is also a working-class community whose members build boats, do construction, and work in the sizeable hospitality industry that reconstitutes itself every summer.

Alan knew that his father, the hockey, football, and baseball coach at Gloucester High School, and his mother, a nurse in a community hospital, made decent money but still lived paycheck to paycheck. He also knew that for some of the parents of his friends, whose work in construction or hospitality was seasonal, the winter months could be extremely tough financially. So Alan went into financial services, with an eye toward serving the blue-collar families in Gloucester he knew so well.

He was so good at what he did that eventually word got around to some of the wealthier residents and summer people. Alan was a wizard with advising, they said. By the time he was forty, Alan essentially had two financial services practices under the same roof—one serving working-class couples and families, the kinds of folks he had grown up with, and the other serving high-net-worth and ultra-high-net-worth individuals and families who were attracted to Alan's thoughtful approach to investing and track record of success.

By the time he was fifty, Alan's firm could have boasted about the success of his practice, had Alan been the boasting type. But that's what the numbers said. Like pretty much everyone else in New England, however, he kept his numbers closely held. He did no marketing or advertising. Whether you were a mechanic or boat builder on the one hand or the heir to a New England manufacturing fortune on the other, you would only learn about Alan's firm by hearing about it from current clients. Alan was so respected that he didn't need to do anything to make the phone ring to attract new clients to his firm.

While "think fast!" might have been the mantra of his childhood, Alan employed exactly the opposite strategy as an investment advisor. He had come to see countless examples of people—rich, middle class, or working class—making snap decisions with their investments, and almost inevitably, those decisions turned out badly. The book that had the greatest impact on Alan was the late Daniel Kahneman's *Thinking, Fast and Slow*. In it, he found a codification of what he had always believed—that the human brain makes decisions in two different ways. Snap decisions—thinking fast—often end badly. On the other hand, thinking slowly about things, taking a rational approach, especially to finance, yielded much better results. Knowing that the brain is responsible for making upward of thirty thousand decisions per day, having two systems for decision-making is only reasonable. While Alan still thought fast in recreational hockey games or while playing ball with his kids, he took a thoughtful and deliberate approach to making decisions when planning his clients' financial futures. Making wise decisions, instead of snap judgments, was the foundation of his success.

It therefore frustrated Alan enormously that when it came to his wealthier clients, they allowed themselves to be driven by unconscious biases or mental shortcuts that inevitably led to losses and sometimes outright disaster. Somehow, his working-class clientele was less susceptible to snap decisions, perhaps because they trusted him more and, by and large, left the decisions to Alan, instead of thinking they themselves were God's gift to financial planning. Alan's high-net-worth clients, by contrast, often believed that since they were rich, they were smart. They allowed those unconscious biases and mental shortcuts to drive the decisions they deemed less complex. And often, as a result, things went down an unintended path.

What kind of biases? Well, to name a few, Alan thought of the following:

- *Recency bias,* meaning that the only evidence people considered was events that had taken place in the recent past. This meant that people were ignoring longer-term trends that actually drove the market or finance in general.
- *Confirmation bias,* meaning that people only wanted to hear and see things that matched up with what they already believed. Alan thought that social media, with its algorithms for feeding people content they would like, only exacerbated that tendency.
- *Overconfidence,* the idea that if I'm good at one thing, I must be good at everything else. *That,* Alan knew, was the ticket to disaster.
- *The gambler's fallacy,* which meant that people saw patterns where none existed. For example, if you are playing roulette and the ball drops onto a red number five times in a row, the gambler's fallacy holds that a black number is "due" to come up. Unfortunately, no such predictions could be made. There was nothing to stop the ball from landing on red a sixth straight time. The so-called law of averages did not apply to a single spin of the roulette wheel, a roll of the dice, or the next card up in a hand of poker or blackjack. And yet people could still find what

they thought was statistical evidence for whatever they wanted to believe—hence the term, the gambler's fallacy.

Alan had seen enough of his high-net-worth and ultra-high-net-worth clients make snap decisions based on these and other mental shortcuts, to the point where they had lost millions of dollars simply because they hadn't thought things through. Alan wanted to see if he could convince some of his clients to learn to "think slow" instead of automatically defaulting to thinking fast. That's when he had the idea for the Lobster League.

Alan invited his high-net-worth and ultra-high-net-worth clients to a weekly discussion group he would lead. The goal would be to have folks talk openly about some of the investment and life decisions made often on the spur of the moment so that he could illustrate for the group the biases that had led to those decisions. Alan thought that by attaching real-life stories of choices, wise and poor, he could make those mental shortcuts or biases evident to all present. While it seemed more difficult for people to notice these forces on their own behavior, maybe if they heard other people's stories, they would understand how common these effects were in everyday life. By becoming more aware of it in others, eventually, they might be more aware of how their own behaviors and decisions were influenced. If they understood the nature of what was driving their decision-making, Alan hoped, they might just stop thinking fast and, instead, take their time and make much more effective, rational decisions.

Here's the note he sent:

Dear [Name of Client], I'm inviting you and a select number of the other top clients of our firm to a unique discussion group that will take place Tuesdays at noon starting Tuesday, September 8, at the Beauport Hotel in Gloucester.

Our goal will be to discuss in an intimate setting financial decisions and critical life decisions—those that worked out great and those that didn't.

We are all subject to certain forms of bias, such as recency bias, overconfidence, a sense of "don't confuse me with the facts," and a half dozen other mental shortcuts that can lead us down the road to ruin.

The only rule of the meeting will be "No judgment!" Everyone who participates will be expected to share a story about a way that they got something very, very right, or very, very wrong, based on a snap judgment. I want folks to see that we all do this, and that there is a better way, which I call Rational Investing.

PS: The Beauport Hotel is renowned for its cuisine, and we will be serving lobster at each lunch. I hope you can join us. Please RSVP below.

Alan had been strategic in his choice of the Beauport Hotel. The hotel had been built less than a decade earlier on the spot where Clarence Birdseye had built his first fish-processing center, making it the birthplace of frozen foods. But that wasn't why Alan chose the hotel. The location was actually a stone's throw from the blue-collar neighborhood where Alan had grown up.

The design of this particular hotel was based on the traditional, sprawling summer hotels of the nineteenth and earlier twentieth centuries, where entire families would come for the whole summer, with dads arriving on the train from Boston each weekend. While the rhythms of life had become far too busy for those sorts of extended trips, the Beauport harkened back to an era when people had the luxury of time and didn't feel constantly harried and harassed by technology as we are today. An environment like that, Alan reasoned, along with its stunning ocean views, might promote the kind of relaxed, rational thinking he was hoping to teach.

Not to mention the fact that their lobster, prepared in a wide variety of ways, was out of this world.

Alan sent the invitations, and within a week, the group was full. First to reply was Gina Thornton, whose late husband, John, had owned the leading boat works in Gloucester. Then came Ed and Susan Farmer. Ed was a top attorney in town, and his wife, Susan, was the assistant principal at Gloucester High School. Next came Natalie Barnes, a divorcee, a retired oboist with the Boston Symphony Orchestra. Then Jane and Mark Darrow came on board. Jane was an accountant, and Mark, unusual for the region, was a stay-at-home dad and multisport coach at nearby Hamilton High School. Liz Stover joined next. Divorced like Natalie, she had never worked, aside from giving piano lessons to local children, often for no charge. She had inherited her family's wealth, which mostly came from buying and holding AT&T stock.

Tracy and David Flynn came on board next. David was a heart surgeon. He and Tracy owned the Breakers, one of the most famous, prestigious, and largest homes in the region. Another couple, Marjorie and Rusty Jenkinson, also joined the group. Marjorie was Mark Darrow's sister, while Rusty owned a very successful HVAC company that he had started when he left the Marines. Rusty was a true "life-of-the-party" guy—you couldn't get married in Gloucester without having Rusty do his famous chicken dance.

The only widower in the group was Phil Barton, who emailed his RSVP next. Phil was a retired judge who had lost his wife to cancer a decade earlier. And finally, Tammy and Fred Thurman filled out the group. The Thurmans ran an accounting firm in Gloucester that they had started twenty-five years earlier. They cross-referred with Alan. Uncommon for Gloucester, the Thurmans were big Vegas people. They loved to go to the casinos and gambling, because both were highly successful card counters. Perhaps that was not a surprise, since they were both great accountants. And unusual for Las Vegas, they won far more often than they lost.

So that was the crew that made up what Alan decided to call the "Lobster League" on account of the fact that lobster would be served at each of the meetings.

A week later, as Alan headed to the Beauport Hotel for the first of those lunches, he had to wonder, *Will people really open up?* Everybody likes to talk about their financial wins, but in a small, tight-knit community like Gloucester, would people be willing to share about the unfortunate decisions they had made?

Well, he decided as he entered the hotel, *if I can teach at least one of these individuals or couples to think slowly instead of thinking fast, the event will be a success.*

But this was New England, home of old money and pursed lips. Would anyone speak up?

Chapter 2

THE OVERCONFIDENT SHIPBUILDER

LOBSTER BISQUE.

The soup was made to perfection by the hotel staff, and all fifteen members of the Lobster League talked excitedly as they enjoyed the delicious repast. The freshest lobster, the best ingredients, savory wine and sherry, fresh cream from a local dairy—shellfish heaven.

As the waitstaff removed the dishes and silverware and brought out coffee and cookies, Alan looked around the room.

"Anyone want to go first?" he asked, scanning the faces of the group members. "Remember. No judgment. And what happens in the Lobster League stays in the Lobster League."

"I'll go," Gina Thornton said, to the surprise of everyone in the room. In a community where people kept their business to themselves, Gina was perhaps the most private person in town. "It's a story I've never wanted to tell."

"Then you've come to the right place," Alan said, and everyone laughed.

"Go for it," Fred Dutton said encouragingly, and his words were met with nods of approval from around the room.

Gina hesitated, and then she leaned forward and began.

"Many of you remember my late husband, John," she said, and the older members of the group nodded respectfully.

"He was a brilliant boat builder," she continued. "Many of your families have sailed on Thornton boats for generations."

A series of nods greeted her statement.

"John came from a long line of master boat builders," she continued. "People around the world would come to Gloucester just to buy his boats. The company dated back to the Revolution. The boatyard employed more than thirty people at its height. John was constantly getting offers from New York to expand. He could have gone from building eight vessels a year to eighty or eight hundred, for all I know. The money people were lined up around the block. Constantly.

"But he was only after one thing. *Quality.* He always said that he could build more boats, but he couldn't put the Thornton name on them. It's not an exaggeration to say that every craft that left that boatyard was built with love."

The nods of approval from those present gave Gina the encouragement to continue telling the story.

"When John turned forty-five," she said, "he had a minor heart attack."

Small gasps met the admission. No one had known that.

"It wasn't serious, thank God," Gina continued. "But it was a wake-up call for John. You could say he was a workaholic, but he would have just described himself as dedicated to his craft. He worked ten to twelve hours a day, six days a week. If I didn't insist that the boatyard be shut for the Lord's Day, he would never have taken a full day off.

"Anyway, our kids were still young. John Jr. was thirteen. None of them particularly liked spending Saturdays at the boatyard, running errands, or learning how to use the tools. John didn't believe that any of the kids wanted any part of the boatyard, and he didn't want to risk keeling over with a lathe in his hands. So that's when he decided to sell."

"I never knew that," Ed Farmer said, fascinated.

"John was a very private person," Gina continued, nodding at Ed. "He would never have wanted his personal business bandied about. That's why I feel somewhat conflicted about telling the story. But I suppose I'm the oldest here. If I don't tell the full truth, I don't know who will. Just trying to set a good example for you young'uns."

Everyone laughed, considering that the youngest person present, aside from Alan, was Jane Farmer, fifty-five years old.

"So he called in one of those dreaded financiers from New York," Gina continued, "And he made a deal. Private equity. They sold that boatyard for a king's ransom."

Gina, being a dyed-in-the-wool New Englander, was not about to quote numbers, but all present knew that the boatyard had to have sold for at least $50 million.

"So now John and I are financially set for life," Gina said, shrugging, as if even that much of an admission went against Yankee values. "So what do you think he did?"

She looked down around the room as if she were about to tell a really funny story.

"He bought a boat!"

Everybody laughed. Of course! What else would a guy like John do?

"It was an eighty-six-foot luxury vessel. John hated the word *yacht*—he thought it sounded pretentious—but this boat was so big, there was no place to dock it in Gloucester. He kept it down in Beverly. Partly because that's the only place in the area with a dry dock big enough, and partly because, well, he didn't want any of you to know just how big a toy he had bought himself."

The room laughed again.

"He just didn't want to have to take us for rides," Ed said, and everyone cracked up.

"Just you, Ed," Gina said, a twinkle in her eye, and the room laughed again.

"So now," she continued, "instead of spending ten hours a day, six days a week at the boatyard, John is down in Beverly, seven days. There was nothing on God's green earth I could do to keep that man away from that boat. It was his absolute pride and joy. It wasn't seaworthy when he bought it, but it was the most beautiful thing you'd ever seen once he got through with it.

"And that's when he took the family across the Atlantic. We summered in Ireland, living on the boat, docking wherever we could find space. Finally, he broke down and rented a smaller vessel, because he realized that all of the little towns he wanted to visit, including the town his family came from, had no facilities for a boat this size. I'm bogging down in details. I'm sorry."

"No," Alan assured her. "We are all loving it. Take your time."

Gina nodded gratefully at Alan and continued.

"After that summer," she said, "we sailed home, and he kind of lost interest in the boat. He's not somebody who sits still very easily. So after taking it down the Intercoastal a couple of times, he sold it, really on a whim, to a South American he met on the dock at Miami who admired the boat. The guy just wrote him a check on the spot, and that was that. He took the boat, the crew, the furniture, all of it. John made a tidy sum on the sale—I'm convinced there might have been some alcohol involved in the negotiations."

The room erupted in laughter again.

"But now we flew home from Miami, and John has literally got nothing to do. And for a man of action like that, idle hands literally were the devil's playground. And this is where the trouble started."

The mood in the room changed as Gina's facial expression shifted from one of happy reminiscence to discomfort and pain.

"A lot of his friends have made great money building houses," she said, her tone somewhat more muted now. "So naturally John thought, *Why can't I?* He figured that if he was good at boats, he would be good at condos. It's just construction, right?

"Well, in some ways he was right, and in others, he was wrong. He had no trouble building the condos. It's a very beautiful community set on farmland just outside Hamilton. He had the devil's own time getting the zoning handled, but once that was taken care of, he built twenty beautiful, luxurious condos. Every amenity you could think of. It was like he was building twenty beautiful boats. He had even poached a couple of his best woodworkers from the shipyard to put in the kitchens, the wainscoting, and the rest of the details."

"I remember what happened next," Fred interjected.

Gina nodded sadly.

"Just as he was about to put the condos on the market," Gina continued, "the market turned against him. All of you remember the Great Recession. For two and a half years, you couldn't get financing for anything under the sun. The carrying costs on the units were just unbelievable. I figured we would just weather the storm. What I didn't know was that John had sunk practically every dollar he had received for the sale of the boatyard into the building of the condos.

"Oh, there were a couple of million left, but he had taken every dime from that sale and sunk it into the real estate deal. When the loan was called, due to the credit squeeze, he lost everything. He couldn't refinance. In the blink of an eye, John lost sixty million dollars."

The room went silent. No one had any idea that the financial hit had been so great.

"John was so dismayed at what had happened," Gina continued sadly, "that he began to drink. And he had never been much of a drinker. He said it interfered with having a clear head for work the next day. But now the drinking increased to the point where he was just gone, around the clock. There was no talking to him. The kids couldn't get through to him. I couldn't. No one could.

"I tried to reason with him and explained that it was only money; we were still perfectly fine. We never aspired to the lifestyle of the super-rich, or at least I certainly didn't. I never knew that he did. He used to scoff at some of our clients who seemed obsessed with having one of his boats as a status symbol, not just something to enjoy with one's family.

"Something changed at some point, I guess, once he had all those zeroes to his net worth. And then one night, after all of us had gone to bed . . ."

Gina's voice trailed off. The room was utterly silent.

"I heard a gunshot from downstairs. When I came down, I saw that John had taken his own life."

The room went ashen. For the longest time, no one spoke.

"That's the saddest story I ever heard," Tammy Thornton said through muffled tears.

"We told everyone that it was a heart attack," Gina said, "but it was no heart attack. It wasn't just that he lost the money. It's that the shipyard had been in the family for generations. He was beside himself because he had destroyed his own patrimony. That was the piece that took him down.

"So now you know." Gina leaned back slightly, as if to indicate that she was done telling the story.

"Thank you, Gina," Alan said quietly. "We're all sorry for your loss, and we're all touched by your enormous courage in sharing this story with us. You've certainly given the rest of the group permission to tell about their own experiences."

Gina nodded quickly to acknowledge Alan's words.

"What John did," Alan continued, looking around the room, "is not uncommon. He took his sense of shame about it, obviously, to a much greater degree than most. But his story illustrates one of the fallacies in thinking that I wanted to share with the group. It's the idea that 'If I'm good at one thing, I'm probably just as good at everything else.'"

All eyes were on Alan now as he continued his explanation.

"As I said last week, there are two kinds of thinking. There's the short-term thinking that's influenced by the sorts of biases we will be examining in the weeks to come, starting today, of course.

"And then there's the second type of thinking, which is rooted in reason as opposed to emotion. It's less susceptible to bias. And ultimately, that's what I'm hoping to share with all of you in this group. That's why I started the group." Alan looked around the room, pulled in the gaze of each person present before moving on to the next.

"We call this type of thinking, very simply, *overconfidence*. Success breeds confidence. What happened with John is as natural as can be. He was highly successful, he had confidence in himself, and he thought his confidence would extend to other areas. Indeed, had the market not turned against him, he probably would have doubled his money. He just had the misfortune of timing not being on his side."

Gina was quietly dabbing at her eyes with a handkerchief she had retrieved from her purse.

"There's nothing wrong with confidence," Alan continued. "If anything, it just makes sense that a man who is good at building one thing would consider himself good at building something else. And as I understood Gina's story, he was very good at building the condos. The error in judgment, if I may speak frankly, is that his overconfidence created a blind spot in understanding the risk he was assuming."

"That was John," Gina said quietly. "He thought he could do anything. Even when the economy turned down, there was no end to the demand for his boats. Not so with condos."

"It's understandable," Alan replied gently. "Forces like an economic downturn were things that he thought did not affect him. He may not have even seen them as risk. John was correctly confident in his ability to build. He was overconfident in his ability to control the elements of the market that were beyond his ability to manage—specifically, the world economy."

The laughter broke the tension.

"He was good, but he wasn't that good," Gina agreed, smiling as she wiped away tears.

"We're all taught to be confident," Alan continued. "And it's good and appropriate that we are confident. We have to feel good about ourselves, and we have to respect our own abilities and talents. Otherwise, we'll never take any risks. We'll never get married. We'll never have children. We'll never start a business. We'll never grow the business we've started.

"But it's all too human to slip from confidence into overconfidence," Alan cautioned. "Confidence is a wonderful thing. But overconfidence is an inaccurate reading of our own skills, and a belief system that tells us that we have no limits. The Wright Brothers had confidence when they took to the air. Icarus, who preceded the Wright Brothers into the sky by thousands of years, had overconfidence. He flew too close to the sun, his wax wings melted, and he fell back to earth. And I'm afraid that's what happened to John."

"Doesn't make him a bad person," Phil Barton said.

"Not in the least!" Alan exclaimed. "It makes him a very human person. We can cross the line from confidence to overconfidence without even realizing it. I never knew John, but my sense is that, as evidenced by the way he did that deal to sell the boat in Miami, he wasn't one for taking too much advice. Is that a fair assessment, Gina?"

"He never looked before he leaped," Gina replied, nodding. "That was part of his charm. It's also what took him down."

"Overconfidence," Alan said. "It's a bias in our thinking that we all need to guard against. Gina, thank you for being so open with the story, and I'm hoping that all of you will respect her privacy, and John's, by not sharing this story with others."

"The cat's out of the bag," Gina said, shaking her head. "At this point, I don't care who knows it. When the kids turned eighteen, I told them. I feel better knowing the secret is out."

"You've got guts," Alan told Gina admiringly. "And you've gotten the Lobster League off to a really great start. Who's ready for dessert?"

Chapter 3

THE HERDING FARMERS

WHEN THEY reunited the following Tuesday, the entire group was buzzing with anticipation. The first meeting had proved a great success, resulting in strong feelings of camaraderie and kinship amongst the clients, establishing they were all safe to share with one another their uncomfortable failings, their embarrassing blunders, their head-smacking gaffs, completely free of judgment or condescension. And now with the freshman jitters out of the way, there was nothing but optimism coloring their sophomore lunch at the Beauport Hotel. Everyone was in good spirits and enthusiastic to continue on their adventure together.

As they were shown to the rear deck, they found the patio space quiet and serene, with few other guests about and a warm breeze gently stirring the leaves of the potted arborvitae, the hems of the blue parasols. A breathtaking panorama of Gloucester

Harbor lay beyond, blue skies with not a single cloud showing, and upon the surface of the water, the noonday sun glinted and shimmered like thousands of floating white diamonds.

The food, as always, was second to none. This week, Alan had arranged for the league to be served Lobster Newberg, a rich dish comprised of sautéed lobster covered in a velvety cream sauce, made of eggs and brandy and seasoned with lemon juice, paprika, and cayenne pepper. Accompanying the group were also several bottles of Prosecco, all chilled in sterling ice buckets placed around the table.

As their meal wound down and their plates were cleared, with the group all leaning back in their seats, satisfied, Alan glanced around the table with an expectant look on his face, and soon the conversation drew to a silence. The clients all glanced at one another, all of them smiling, and a few began laughing for the anticipatory excitement lingering in the air.

"Last week, everyone was too nervous to speak up," said Alan. "Now everyone's afraid of appearing overeager."

The group all laughed.

"We don't mind appearing eager," said Susan Farmer, glancing over at her husband with a smile.

Ed Farmer shook his head. "Not at all," he said. "If the rest of you don't mind?"

The table did not and encouraged the Farmers to go on. Susan looked to her husband again, and he smiled at her, topped up both of their Proseccos, and then leaned back, letting Susan take the reins.

"Ed and I have been married for thirty-five years," began Susan. "He's an attorney with Asner & Associates, and I'm the assistant principal over at Gloucester High. So we've always been quite secure. Perhaps not as secure as several of you . . ."

The group chuckled.

". . . but we've always been comfortable. A solid pension, savings, our kids are established. Everything set up nicely for our coming retirement. But we realized several years ago that we didn't really have much in the way of investments. A few mutual funds, blue chips, but nothing substantial. A number of our friends had also mentioned how lucrative their returns had been on their own investments in the last few years. And these weren't especially knowledgeable people either, mind you, but their ROIs were hard to ignore. So we thought why not? We figured we'd earn a bit extra and be able to afford the finer things in life."

"Well, *one* finer thing," said Ed, with a smile.

Susan looked at him and gestured for him to continue.

"The Brookside House," said Ed, turning to the group. "Located just south of Essex. A beautiful old Queen Anne estate. It had been the familial home of my ancestors for generations before being lost in a nasty divorce settlement with one of my great uncles."

"We don't speak of that," joked Susan.

"Well, Susan and I had discovered—this was several years ago now—that the owner of the home had been failing to pay property taxes and that there was likely going to be a tax lien foreclosure by the city. I won't bore you with the details, but I'd always dreamed of owning that house, of bringing it back into my family, and Susan couldn't have been more supportive, saying we should go after it if it ever got put up for auction. Despite her also saying that the estate reminded her of the Bates House from *Psycho*."

The group laughed again.

"It really did," said Susan.

"And so I just couldn't find a reason *not* to double-down on our investments at this time. Not least because I knew that if I didn't buy the Brookside, it was eventually going to be destroyed."

"Destroyed?" said Natalie Barnes, one of the two divorcees in the group.

"A hawkish property developer had already bought up a few places in the area," said Ed. "He was with some predatory firm who'd begun tearing down all the old houses to prepare for some new business endeavor. A golf course or something like that. I didn't pay too much attention at the time. But I knew that Brookside didn't stand a chance if this developer were able to outbid me at auction. So we needed that little extra."

"Really, the house was just one of several reasons we wanted to invest further," said Susan. "The big-ticket item, sure, but mostly we just wanted to have more security. To set up trusts for our children, our grandchildren, that kind of thing."

"And so?" said Natalie.

"And so we did it," said Susan. "We jumped in head first and hooked up with a financial advisor our friends had recommended, explicitly telling him that we only wanted to invest in growth stocks."

"Why only growth stocks?" said Phil Barton, the widower.

Ed shrugged. "Because that's what all our friends had done. They said it was the smart way to go."

"Oh, how I wish you'd called me first," said Alan.

The table laughed.

"Trust me: So do we," said Ed.

"But it went really well," said Susan. "For a while, at least. Better than we had anticipated. We were seeing steady returns, planning for our future, and Ed was keeping an eye on the Brookside, waiting on the day he'd hear the treasurer had begun foreclosure proceedings. And reviewing our finances one particular February, we just couldn't believe our luck as the stock market was on a historic run. That was, of course, until . . ."

Susan cut herself off and lowered her head, letting out a deep, frustrated exhalation. Ed reached out and took her hand in his and squeezed gently, comforting her, and after a moment he finished her thought.

"It was February 2020," he said.

The table all let out a knowing sigh.

"We had no idea what was coming for us," said Ed. "I suppose neither did anyone else."

"That Black Monday in March saw the largest single-day point drop in the Dow's history," said Susan. "It was just awful."

"It lost close to eight percent. Thirty-five percent over that month."

"So we, of course, were panicking. Just like everybody else. Our financial advisor kept reassuring us that the market would bounce back eventually, but we just couldn't hear him. It was all so surreal. I mean, everyone here must remember that period, right? Those first few weeks of COVID. Quarantining, lockdowns, dead city streets."

"Toilet-paper barons," joked Ed.

"It felt like the end of the world. Truly. *Unprecedented times.* And so on top of everything else, we just couldn't handle the pressure of seeing our investments dwindle down to nothing. And every one of our friends had already started to pull out. The ones who'd gotten us to invest further in the first place. They thought we were crazy for holding on as long as we did, which was only perhaps a week or so longer than them. But I mean, literally *everyone* was selling off. The whole world was. And what did we know? We were just so new to the whole experience."

"I remember we were waking up every day to check the Dow, the S&P 500, only to find that they'd sunk even further," said Ed. "It was a terrible feeling. I had an instinct to hold, with my conscience telling me that sooner or later things would turn around. That nothing lasts forever. But that was just such a crazy period. Everything was uncertain. A friend of ours, an old law school classmate, he actually even sat me down at one point to try and talk some sense into me, as he put it."

"Mm," said Susan, remembering.

"He told me, he said, Ed, listen, we're all really worried about you and told me that he'd talked with all our close friends—"

"All of whom had already sold off, mind you."

"That's right. All had sold. And so he's telling me this, that he's seen this kind of behavior before, that I had a big problem on my hands, and I'm honestly starting to feel like I was at my own intervention or something. He said he knew how I felt, but that it was strictly a male ego thing, that I was just being prideful. That I needed to join the others and sell off immediately. I remember he mentioned BlackBerry, about how they'd refused to pivot after the release of the iPhone, refusing to admit that touchscreens were the future of the market, and that they'd done so simply out of stubbornness and pride. And because of their egos, my friend said, their billion-dollar empire was reduced to nothing very quickly, their share of the global smartphone market dwindling down to less than one percent."

"So obviously," said Susan, "Ed and I felt like our backs were against the wall. And so we sold. What else could we do? We followed our friends' advice. And, well, I'm sure most of you know what happened after that."

"The market rebounded," said Alan, a sympathetic look on his face.

"Boy, did it ever," said Susan. "And very quickly too, in just a few months. By mid-summer, the stimulus checks were being dished out, there were lower interest rates, and things really started to shift."

"And by the end of the year," said Ed, "the S&P 500 and the Nasdaq had both in fact not just rebounded, but had reached all-time highs. Yet another unprecedented event."

"But by that time, we'd long since pulled it all," said Susan.

"Everything?" said Natalie.

"Everything. All of it."

"Our advisor tried to ease us back into investing again," said Ed, "even by late that summer, but we were just way too gun shy to jump back in at that point."

Ed turned and looked out over the water, seeming to grow almost wistful. Beyond could be seen the historic Ten Pound Island Lighthouse, a flock of ivory gulls circling overhead, and Ed appeared to be staring at them as if they held some answer.

"And by that point . . ." he said, trailing off.

Susan looked at him and took his hand and lovingly patted the top of it. Ed turned to her, now released from his reverie, and gave an appreciative smile. He looked back around the table.

"By that point the city had foreclosed on the Brookside," he said, "and put the house up for auction."

A long silence rose among the group.

"And did you bid?" said Phil Barton.

"No," said Ed. "We just couldn't afford to. And when we found out what the winning bid actually was, we were completely heartbroken. It was much lower than we'd anticipated. We would've been better off if we'd never invested the money in the first place."

A collective sigh passed around the table. Some of the group shaking their heads, some briefly reflecting upon the tragic vicissitudes of their own lives. After a moment, Phil spoke again, yet he was already surmising the answer he'd receive before he even asked the question.

"And who won the house?" he asked.

Susan let out a bitter laugh and Ed looked over at her and smiled, reassuring her that he was all right, that he'd made peace with what had occurred. Then he looked back at Phil and smiled all the same and yet every single member at that table could see plain as day that he carried the hurt with him still.

"The hawkish property developer won," said Ed.

Phil nodded, his hunch now proved correct, and he looked at Ed with an anticipatory expression on his face. Another question bubbling under the surface.

"Go on," said Ed. "It's all right."

"What happened to the house?" said Phil.

Ed took a moment to respond, collecting himself further. This was indeed the bitterest of all pills to swallow. Then he cleared his throat, took a drink of Prosecco, and answered.

"The Brookside was torn down last summer," he said.

A hushed gasp sounded around the table.

"To be replaced with a shopping mall," said Susan, her tone acidic. "If you can believe it."

"A *shopping mall*?" said Natalie.

"It seems that antiquated notions aren't the sole dominion of BlackBerry," said Ed, causing a swell of laughter around the table. A much-needed dose of levity.

"We later severed ties with our old advisor and hooked up with Alan," said Ed. "And he helped us better align our investments with our goals, which was something we'd never experienced before. Taught us more than a thing or two. And indeed things have been going very well ever since."

"He's held our hands tightly throughout the process this time around," said Susan. "Much tighter than I'm sure he's comfortable with."

Alan laughed.

"But the whole ordeal was just . . ."

"An eye-opener," said Ed.

"Yes. Exactly," said Susan. "An eye-opener. It's taken us a couple years to get over all of it. Not just the loss of the house, but I think more so that awful feeling of realizing how foolish you'd been."

"It's perfectly natural," said Alan. "What you two fell into. The timeless trap of: *Everyone else is doing it, so it must be right.*"

Alan glanced around at the other members. "How many times have we all thought that?" he said.

The group all nodded, letting out various affirmations.

"It's helpful to remember that it isn't *always* a terrible maxim," said Alan. "In fact, it can sometimes be a very helpful one. When in Rome, do as the Romans do, right? But when it comes to important life decisions, particularly with investments, we need to make sure we take time to consider all the options in front of us, consider all the facts, and not just the ones our friends have curated for us."

Alan took a drink and then leaned forward, looking at the Farmers.

"The concept is known as *herding*," he said. "An extremely common behavior."

Ed and Susan lowered their gaze and Alan could sense their shame and made to qualify his comments.

"There's nothing to be embarrassed about," he said. "Sincerely. Look, you behaved the way that the vast majority of the world did. Like you said, there were millions of people selling off in March 2020. It's just social proof. If the guy next door appears to have more experience, seems more knowledgeable than you on a certain issue, well, then it only makes sense to mirror his behavior. The problem, however, is that often these so-called knowledgeable people are anything but. I find your law school friend's example of BlackBerry, his accusations of prideful behavior, particularly illuminating. Because—and if you'll forgive me for being critical of your friend . . ."

"Don't be," said Susan. "The both of us sure have been."

"Well, it seems to me that *he*, in fact, was the one being prideful in that particular situation. He demonstrated arrogance by condescending to you. By being certain that he had all the answers when, as would become clear later on, he absolutely did not. Your actions, on the other hand, were thoughtful and considerate. Measured. You wanted to take a moment to weigh the pros and cons of your decision, all the while the world was spinning out of control—which takes fortitude. That starts with being really clear about what you're trying to accomplish. When you're clear about your goals, you can align your investment choices with appropriate investments. Short-term goals are very different than long-term, with regard to what investments match achieving them. You two should indeed be proud of yourselves for resisting as long as you did. Herding is an incredibly compelling behavior and what makes it so widespread.

"Now, I want to stress that the concept of herding is not some hard-science fact," said Alan. "It's just a particular term that's been arrived at over the years that effectively describes a behavior almost every single one of us engages in on a daily basis. It is something that provides psychological safety and comfort. And this is indeed one of the most common behaviors when it comes to investing. But it is an *emotional* response, not a logical one, and therefore it's something that needs to be mitigated when making important decisions.

"Because herding all too often becomes a self-fulfilling prophecy. When people buy a stock, the stock price goes up, and so other people take notice and buy the stock themselves and it goes up further, and so on and so on. But this can go the other way too, of course. When a stock price drops, people start selling off, and the stock drops further, and then even more people sell. I often think that people forget what *buy low, sell high* actually means. It means sometimes buying when the stock is ostensibly not doing very well, when it indeed appears that buying is the completely *wrong* decision to make. Now, of course, it can be wrong in a lot of cases—what we call a *falling-knife* scenario. Anyone here buying BlackBerry shares lately?"

The group all chuckled.

"But something like the market crash of 2020 is a different story," said Alan. "A crash represents panic. It represents illogical thinking, *emotional* decision-making, though it can also sometimes be one of the most opportune times to buy. Stocks will certainly be at their lowest during the nadir of a crash, but very often the market bounces back. Which means those stocks that you bought at low prices will soon be worth much, much more. And then you complete the process, selling off when they're at their highest, after the market rallies, as it did by the end of 2020. That's what we call rebalancing. Something most people don't do.

"But most people simply follow the momentum of the market. They don't consider the broader picture. If the market's down, people get out. If it's up, people buy in. *This* is herding. When you're selling low and buying high. And as I like to say: Herding means hurting."

He turned and looked at the Farmers once more.

"If I can just say this too—I don't know who your previous financial advisor was, but he did you two an absolute disservice. The fact that you wanted to get into the market short-term, to buy a house, that you were only getting in because your friends were—these are all red flags and should have been addressed immediately by your advisor.

"So you two really have no reason to be so hard on yourselves," he said. "You've learned a valuable lesson about investing and about life in general: The herd is often wrong. And now, having been through your difficult experience, you've become much more knowledgeable about how investing works, haven't you? The next time you feel panicked about an investment decision, you'll be able to stop, step back, and assess the situation effectively. *Am I making a logical decision here or am I just going with the herd?* And if you realize you *are* going with the herd, well, then, just give me a call and we'll sort it out."

Ed and Susan smiled warmly at him and thanked him for his comments and for his guidance, and Alan assured them it was his pleasure.

"Well then," Alan said, switching gears. "Are we ready for coffee?"

He turned to their waiter standing on the other side of the patio and signaled him over.

Chapter 4

HARMONY AND STRENGTH

THE LIGHT aroma of garlic and basil filled the air, lobster ravioli on the menu this week, and the table all looked on with excitement as their servers set their meals before them. Golden handcrafted *pasta all'uovo* pockets filled with buttery lobster meat and silky ricotta cheese, simmered until al dente, then coated with a saffron-infused cream sauce and finished with a crumble of crispy pancetta, drizzled truffle oil, and dusted parmesan cheese. Another masterful dish prepared by the brilliant Beauport Hotel chef.

When they'd finished, Alan glanced around the table and caught the eyes of Natalie Barnes staring back at him. She'd been waiting for him to look over, and by the glint in her eye, Alan could tell she was keen to be the day's speaker. He smiled and nodded in acknowledgment, and Natalie dabbed the sides of her mouth with her napkin before taking a drink of water, preparing to speak.

"Natalie," said Alan, "would you like to share this week?"

"If I may?" said Natalie, glancing around at the others. There were no objections.

She then looked to the Farmers sitting across from her. "Ed and Susan's story last week," she said, "their touching upon the pandemic, it made me think . . . well, COVID hit us all, didn't it? In myriad ways."

"Go on," said Alan. "The floor is yours."

The rest of the group all turned to Natalie, their servers now clearing the lunchware from the table, and Natalie straightened up in her seat slightly and cleared her throat. She was an elegant and decorous woman, sixty-nine-years old, dressed in a bespoke blue blazer and white blouse with a dotted silk ascot around her neck. Adorned in pearl stud earrings and a sailboat brooch, she also wore a signet ring with her family crest engraved upon it.

She folded her napkin over once, twice, and then set it aside as if clearing the clutter from her tribune, and even in this simple gesture she demonstrated herself a woman of efficient motion. All her movements full of grace and composure.

"Hello, everyone," she said, her mouth curling slightly.

The group smiled back, returning the hello.

"I know we've all been introduced already, but just in case any of you forgot, my name is Natalie Barnes. At my age, memory's about as reliable as the weather. And even then, it's often a wild nor'easter."

The table all laughed.

"I'm a musician," continued Natalie. "Well, a retired musician. I was principal oboist with the Boston Symphony Orchestra. And what a charmed life that was. To solo on Strauss's Oboe Concerto at Tanglewood, to tour around the country, the world, performing at Carnegie Hall, the Kennedy Center. I recorded several pieces under the direction of the brilliant Seiji Ozawa. Prokofiev, Ravel, Bach. It was a dream, really. A glowing, brilliant, eight-year-old fantasy come true.

"Music has always been in my blood, you see. Literally. Us Barneses coming from a long line of musicians, stretching back several centuries at least. All the way back to old world Glasgow. Sir Henry Barnes, my great-great-great- . . . well, I can't actually remember how many greats it is."

The group chuckled.

"There's that nor'easter blowing right on through," joked Natalie. "But it doesn't matter. My very great-grandfather Henry Barnes was a minstrel and court musician in the sixteenth century. Indeed he was the royal lutist to King James. And he traveled all over Europe, seeking new sounds, new compositions, before he eventually sailed here to the New World. He settled in Plymouth where he continued to perform, his offspring following suit, and over the years, his ancestors slowly started to spread north to Boston, Salem, Gloucester. Onward to Vermont and Maine. His two sons were fiddlers and they made a living playing folk music at church services and local dances, contributing to the family's growing reputation, with one of the grandsons later composing symphonies for orchestras in New York and Philadelphia. Many more composers, conductors, and opera singers followed. And whether classical, folk, or jazz—we did it all. Still today there are dozens of Barneses in the music industry, all over the world. Performers and producers and coaches."

She smiled self-consciously, realizing she was getting off topic, and she took another drink of water.

"Forgive me," she said. "I can ramble from time to time. All that is to say that my family has been here, playing music, for a long, long time. Our family motto indeed reflecting our lineage of musicality and unity. Of the sum being more than their parts."

She held up her signet ring for the table to see, flashing her family crest.

"Harmonia et Fortitudo," she said. "Harmony and Strength."

After a moment, she glanced down at the crest herself.

"These virtues became deeply meaningful to me as I grew older. They were traits I looked for and found in my husband, Benjamin. In our relationship. The two of us together, harmonious and strong. It's why I married him."

She looked back at the group.

"He was a financial advisor. The CFO for the Atlantic Fisheries corporation. A beautiful man. Elegant and worldly. He reminded me of Cary Grant."

The group smiled.

"We were very dissimilar in a lot of ways—myself the more creative, musical, right-brain type and he the analytical, mathematical left-brain—but I think that's what made it work. We completed one another. And what a beautiful life he made for me. He always made it so that I wanted for nothing. Never once did I worry about our finances, our savings, none of that. He allowed me to focus solely on my music. And I see now what an absolute luxury that was. What a gift.

"Anyway, as the both of us neared retirement, Benjamin found us a gorgeous summer home in Rockport that we began frequenting every weekend. A beautiful spot overlooking the ocean with a giant wraparound porch, a fieldstone firepit. The bedroom faced the east and every morning we'd rise early, the two of us nestled into one another, holding hands as the sky blushed out over the water. Watching the world begin. Benjamin told me those were his favorite moments. Just lying there, watching the sun rise. And I have to admit they were my favorite too."

Natalie cleared her throat, overwhelmed with emotion, before she continued on.

"But one morning, five years ago now, there at the Rockport house, Benjamin woke up feeling just dreadful," she said. "As if he'd come down with the worst flu of his life, he said. And it persisted for several days until we went to the doctor to get him checked out, and there he was diagnosed with COVID-19."

The group all sighed with great sympathy. Natalie glanced across the table at the Farmers again, and Ed and Susan looked back at her with expressions of deep compassion on their faces. Aware now that her COVID-related loss cut much deeper than their own.

"It was terrible news," said Natalie. "Obviously. This was February 2020, so we hadn't even heard of COVID by that point, but the doctor explained that it was quite serious, especially for Benjamin. He was seventy-two at the time, diabetic, and had suffered from asthma all his life, so he was not in a good spot. Though we were told not to worry too much, that most cases turned around on their own. To just self-isolate and make sure Benjamin got enough rest.

"But things only got worse. He developed a fever and started to become short of breath and indeed within days of returning from the doctor, I took him to the hospital, he was wheezing so bad. I thought it was just a precautionary step—I mean, he'd had asthmatic fits before—but very quickly it became apparent that something was very wrong. He was soon given oxygen therapy and fluids to prevent dehydration, the doctors were keeping him under close observation, and very soon they'd begun giving him steroids to try and bring down the inflammation in his lungs and . . ."

Natalie cut herself off, clearly affected by her memories of that time, and she turned her head to the side. She removed a silk handkerchief from her blazer pocket, folded it over twice, and dabbed at the corners of her eyes before returning it. Then she took another drink of water and continued.

"A few days after he was hospitalized, things became critical," she said. "Benjamin's lungs began to struggle to function properly and he was moved to the ICU where he was placed on a ventilator. There were doctors and nurses checking his vitals around the clock, life support and advanced care options now being discussed. It was all just so awful. And that went on for several weeks without improvement. Up until the moment the doctor told me that he'd likely never recover. I'll never forget it. Even if I was willing to sign off on more aggressive treatment options, they said at Benjamin's advanced age, it was very unlikely that he'd survive. And then discussions turned to palliative care."

A long silence followed, with Natalie taking some time to compose herself, to muster her strength.

"I took Benjamin home," she said, "to our house in Rockport. I didn't want his final moments spent in some hospital bed, so we had everything set up in our bedroom there in Rockport, all the machines, everything he needed. A nurse would come by every day and check up on him. Help make him as comfortable as possible. The worst part about everything was that though he could barely speak at that point, I could see in his eyes that he was still all there. Still the same Benjamin that I'd always known. And it was torturous seeing him like that. Caged by his own body. Trapped. I don't know if any of you have ever read *Johnny Got His Gun*, but . . .

"Well, his breath had really started to slow that last night. But he held on. And I know now that he held on for me. He held on until the morning. And there, in bed in our little spot hidden away from the world, the two of us holding hands, I nestled into him and we watched the sky blush out over the ocean, watched the sun rise together, one final time."

All around the table the league stared back at Natalie with looks of condolence and immense feeling upon their faces. A few wiping tears from their eyes. Gina Thornton, sat directly beside Natalie, indeed now began sobbing into her napkin, and Natalie soon reached over and took her hand to comfort her.

"I'm sorry, Gina," she said. "I—"

"No," said Gina, collecting herself. "Thank you, but you have nothing to be sorry about. Thank you for sharing that with us. It's nice to know that I'm not alone. That you and I are . . . bonded."

Natalie squeezed her hand and gave a bittersweet smile and Gina smiled back. Then Natalie turned back to the table.

"After Benjamin passed, I was a complete mess," she said. "I just felt so adrift, so lost, and for a couple of years afterward, really. But eventually I pulled myself together. I started volunteering, filling my days up, seeing friends, and soon enough I was able to move forward. Never forgetting, of course. Never going more than an hour without thinking about him, without missing him, but continuing on. Living. And I discovered then that Benjamin had set things up for me financially so that I'd be well taken care of. Not that this was surprising—he *always* made sure I was taken care of—but it was a great comfort. A weight off my shoulders. I discovered we had a significant amount in cash as well as a robust stock portfolio. And besides that I had my pension, Social Security, so I thought, financially at least, I'm fine. We'd always done well for money before, so I figured I'd do well forever, you know? And so I did nothing with our portfolio, I didn't even look at it. I just continued on with Benjamin's investments. And the portfolio had done well, even in 2022, which I'm told was a bad year. I'd check our returns every so often and they continued to grow, so what else could I say? If it ain't broke, don't fix it."

The group chuckled.

"In hindsight, I realize just how naive a mindset that really was," said Natale. "I mean, I wouldn't even glance at anything pre-COVID. To see how my portfolio had done over the last five, let alone ten years. To me, it was: Benjamin took care of everything before, so my job was to take care of everything *now*. That's it. Why should I be concerned with anything other than what's happened in the past couple years? And, like I said, things were going well in that regard. Up until the moment that they weren't.

"You see, Benjamin had most of our investments tied up in just a few stocks. Stocks that had been historically sound.

Household names that had been around for a long time. Well, for various reasons, the majority of these stocks started to sink last year. Our large portfolio very quickly dwindled down. It was shocking to me. All I'd ever seen was our savings grow. I'd always had money and so I always *would* have money, right? Or so I thought. But with our portfolio reduced to nearly nothing and the large amount in cash Benjamin had set aside disappearing much quicker than I had anticipated, I soon started to realize that if I didn't do something fast I was going to be in big trouble. And I still had a lot of life to live, as far as I was concerned. I appreciate none of you snickering at my saying that, by the way."

The group laughed again.

"And so I reached out to Alan," said Natalie, "and I told him that I needed help. And God bless him, he made me see that things were much worse than I'd originally thought."

Alan laughed.

"Yes, but you *were* on top of it," he said. "Though you may not have known exactly what was happening, you had sharp enough instincts to realize that you needed assistance. Which can't be said for everybody. Most people just bury their heads in the sand until it's too late."

Alan leaned forward in his seat and glanced around the table.

"Since Benjamin took care of the finances," he said, "Natalie wasn't privy to the ups and downs of the market. And since Benjamin was such a savvy investor, as I would learn going through his materials, he was able to grow their wealth year after year with relative ease. As a CFO and a corporate finance expert, Benjamin understood when changes to his stocks needed to be made. Natalie was completely unaware that this was being done or even how to do it. As Natalie puts it, the numbers kept going up. Even after he passed, his investments were still bearing fruit, and so Natalie didn't personally experience any financial downturns, nor even see that as a possibility. It just wasn't part of her investment experience. And this is what is known as recency bias. *If things have been great, then they'll continue to be great, won't they?* Well, unfortunately not. And so it was this recency bias that Natalie and I needed to recalibrate before we could get her back on her feet again. And so we did."

"You told me it's one of the most common reasons for unbalanced portfolios," said Natalie.

"It is," said Alan. "When stocks go up, we're obviously inclined to buy more shares, though this is at the detriment of less glamorous but less riskier investments. Bonds, for example. So when recency bias takes hold, a portfolio of stocks that has been doing well often becomes much riskier overall. Say, for example, you have 50 percent of your money in stocks and 50 percent in cash and bonds. And let's say your stocks do quite well for five years or so. Well, now you start to think that these particular stocks will *always* do well and so you start putting 75 percent of your money into them and reduce your cash and bonds to 25 percent. But if those stocks wind up taking a dive, then you're in a much more vulnerable position than you were before, since three-quarters of your money is now much more volatile. This is especially true if you have a concentrated stock portfolio.

"So when this happened with your own portfolio, Natalie, with Benjamin investing most of your money into these concentrated stocks and keeping the other part in cash, you were quickly thrown into an uncomfortable position. This says nothing of Benjamin's financial acumen, by the way. Obviously he could not have foreseen the coronavirus happening, could not have foreseen getting sick, and no one can predict the future. But things happen. And thanks to your vigilance, we were able to address the issue and turn things around."

"*My* vigilance?" said Natalie. "You're the one who taught me how to refill my bucket. I just sat and listened."

Alan smiled. "You're too modest," he said.

Natalie waved her hand, dismissing this.

"I mean it," said Alan. "Don't sell yourself short. You were laser-focused when you came into my office. You had a problem, and you were going to fix it, and that was the end of it. For every single one of my questions, you had a clear and concise answer. *How much is enough? What's more important: growth or security? How much risk are you comfortable with?* You were prepared for it all. Though you didn't have the tools yet, you had a plan for getting yourself out of your situation. That right-brain creativity working in tandem with your left-brain logic. That old Barnes harmony and strength alive and well."

Natalie smiled warmly at him and Alan smiled back before he turned to the others.

"Recency bias," he said. "It's human nature, simple as that. If things are going well, why rock the boat? Just look at what happened with GE or IBM. Many families held those companies as their only investments in stocks for generations. Or the '08 crash. Pre-crash everyone wanted to own real estate, but post-crash? We can often have very short memories, can't we? I recall Gore Vidal using the term *the United States of Amnesia.*"

The table laughed.

"That was more to do with politics than finance, but you take my point," said Alan. "Just look at any period in history. Today it's NVDIA, Apple, Amazon, Tesla. Those are considered good stocks simply because they've been good recently. But 'good recently' isn't relevant to individual investment choices. Again, it's *What are you looking for with your portfolio? What do you want it to accomplish for you? What kind of risk-security balance do you want?* Remember the famous quote: 'The only constant in life is change.' Yet our brains are not wired for change. Change is scary, and it's easier to avoid most of the time. And that is the trap that people can fall into and why recency bias is so common."

Alan turned to Natalie once more.

"And if I might add one final comment," he said, "you're quite good at it."

Natalie gave a bashful smile. "Good at what?" she said.

"Financial planning. For someone who didn't turn her mind to such things until much later in life, you're a natural. You've picked up on terms and concepts that I've seen chartered analysts bluff their way through. You're inquisitive, you listen. You don't just make a decision—before it's made, you ask yourself, *Why am I making it?* You ask, *What does this do for me?* And your portfolio has seen tremendous success because of it."

Natalie gave another smile. "Thank you, Alan."

"It's been my pleasure."

Their servers approached the table once more and began handing out dessert menus.

"All right then," said Alan, flipping through the menu. "Enough finances for one day. The only numbers that matter now are how many steps it's going to take to walk off this crème brûlée."

Chapter 5
COLD CASH

WHEN THEY congregated the following week, the Lobster League was greeted by yet another balmy summer afternoon. The patio humming with laughter and pleasant conversation, the air filled with the intoxicating aroma of fried clams and baked haddock. Out on the water could be seen several vessels preparing for the upcoming Gloucester Harbor Race, and the league regarded their numbers with quiet repose as they lunched. There were sailboats of every kind, sloops and catamarans, a couple of small racing yachts, and even the grand *Adventure* vessel, a knockabout schooner built nearly a hundred years ago and deemed a National Historic Landmark, cutting through the water as if indeed transported from another time.

The group dined on *royale* lobster rolls that week, a decadent reimagining of the classic seaside handheld, with succulent chunks of lobster poached lightly in beurre monté, dressed in a creamy citrus-saffron aioli, and served on a freshly baked brioche bun toasted golden brown. Garnished with Imperial Osetra caviar and shaved black truffles, the dish was served with a bisque espuma dipping sauce.

As they ate, Jane and Mark Darrow continued to look at the ships out on the harbor, watching a particular cutter yacht set its sails. The white canvas of the giant genoa glowed luminescent beneath the bright midday sun, the cutter gliding smoothly over the waves. A monument to independence, to boundless freedom, to bold new horizons. Jane glanced over at her husband and smiled, and he smiled back, an inside joke passing between them.

"What could have been, huh?" said Mark.

Alan overheard them and playfully raised an eyebrow. "Sounds like there might be a juicy story there," he said.

Jane and Mark laughed.

"Unless I'm prying," said Alan.

"Not at all," said Jane. "Mark and I have just always thought about buying a boat. Ever since we were kids."

"You two still *are* kids as far as the rest of us are concerned," said Natalie Barnes. Jane and Mark were considerably younger than the others, yet in their mid-fifties.

"Well," said Jane with a smile, "Mark and I—"

She stopped herself and looked back across the table at Alan.

"Are you sure I'm not being rude?" she said.

"Rude?" said Alan. "How so?"

"Well, the two of us are here as guests. I've worked with a few around this table in my role as a financial accountant," said Jane, glancing around the group. "Though out of respect, I'll keep their identities a secret."

The group laughed, and Jane glanced across the table at Marjorie Jenkinson, her sister-in-law, and at Marjorie's husband, Rusty. The three sharing a knowing grin between them.

"Respect for who exactly?" joked Rusty. "Yourself or us?"

He looked around the table with mock embarrassment as if he'd accidentally and not intentionally spilled the beans. "Oops," he said.

The table, Jane and Mark included, all laughed together.

"Quiet, you," said Marjorie to her husband. "Loose lips sink ships."

"Well then, thank God they haven't bought the boat yet."

More laughter.

"I suppose we just feel a bit guilty taking time from everyone else," said Jane, looking back at Alan.

"Everyone will have their turn," said Alan. "I promise. So you two just go right on ahead."

A number of the other members voiced their affirmation and encouragement, coaxing the Darrows to continue, and Jane and Mark smiled warmly at one another. They were a handsome couple, Jane exuding a laid-back elegance, effortlessly chic in a lightweight linen blazer and casual silk blouse, with Mark in an open-collar Oxford and dark blue trousers worn over spotless white deck shoes. After a moment, her hesitance laid to rest, Jane then turned back to the table and began.

"All right then," she said. "Well, as I mentioned, I'm an accountant at Harper & Stone, and Mark is a repairman for Crescent Ridge Property Management. Lots of contract work, odd jobs, things like that."

"HIC certified," said Mark, with a faux braggadocio.

"We don't make Lobster League money," said Jane, "but we do all right for ourselves."

The table chuckled.

"We don't have any kids either, so that helps," said Mark. "With finances, I mean."

"And everything else," said Rusty.

More laughter.

"All that being said, we've never been good at spending money," said Jane. "I don't mean that we're reckless, that we're spendthrifts—I mean that we're the exact opposite. We find it very difficult to spend money on anything unless we absolutely have to. And we've appreciated ourselves a substantial amount because of this, so you'd think we'd have loosened up a bit over the years, but no. We still find it impossible to indulge, to get comfortable with big purchases or luxuries of any kind."

"Don't let us be misunderstood," said Mark. "We like nice things, but there's just a deep feeling of regret always hanging over our decision-making process. As if we're being irresponsible or impulsive. *Sure, we can afford it now, but things change, right? What's going to happen down the road? Will we even like this purchase in a month's time? A week's?*"

"But you have been thinking about buying a boat," said Alan.

"Oh, yes," Mark said with a smile. "I've been obsessing over it."

"For how long now?"

Mark glanced sideways at Jane, and they both laughed.

"Since he was three," said Jane.

The table all smiled.

"Oh, but you should see this thing," said Mark. "A forty-footer with a polished teak deck, a mahogany helm, a queen-sized berth in the bow. Every time I look at the brochure, I can almost smell the ocean air, can see Jane and me on the deck watching the sun set out on the water."

"Well, if I might suggest something?" said Alan.

"Please."

"Buy the boat."

The group all laughed.

"I know. I know," said Mark. "We're just . . ."

"We've always been like this," said Jane. "Even before we met one another. We're just always so focused on the risk. Which, to be fair, has served us well in other aspects of our lives. But not when it comes to luxuries."

"We don't come from money," said Mark. "Neither one of us does. Our families were very working class. Very blue collar. Hand to mouth. My father was a custodian who was employed by the Public Works Department, and he spent his entire life trying to take over the small department he worked for. To become the manager of the half-dozen other custodians. Worked himself to the bone, always on call. I barely saw him growing up. And then what happened? Ten years in and they promoted some other guy and that some other guy wound up laying my father off. It was awful. I don't think he ever recovered from that, to be honest. And so I think Jane and I have developed a bit of an impostor syndrome due to our upbringing, to be honest, since we've been able to establish ourselves as affluent. I mean, certainly more affluent than our parents were by a country mile."

"And with no kids," said Rusty and smiled.

"With no kids," said Mark.

"I think we just assumed that those who were truly well-off—those with boat money," smirked Jane, "were those who'd inherited their wealth and not earned it, as ignorant as that sounds. We have savings, we both have solid 401(k)s, but it never felt like *wealth* to us, if that makes any sense. It felt like earnings. Like something else entirely."

"Jane's always been eager for us to invest more," said Mark, "and we have a bit tied up in a few money markets, but I've just always been hesitant about all that stuff. Anytime I look at the stock market, it seems to be in decline, which I know isn't true, but I'm somehow always hearing that *this* stock is down or that *that* stock is down. I think maybe I'm reading the wrong newspapers."

The table laughed.

"For me, there's just always this nagging concern in the back of my mind that the next contract won't come," said Mark. "That some storm is coming in and it's going to wipe us out completely, and I'll be left unemployed and penniless like my father was."

"We're timid and gun-shy, and then we're surprised down the road when we haven't accumulated a larger nest egg," said Jane. "Honestly, just like Mark, some days I worry I'll wind up like my own father. He was a lovely man, kind-hearted, but he was also a complete miser."

Mark laughed to himself and nodded his head.

"He'd track every dollar he spent," said Jane, "literally writing it down in a little notebook with his tiny little handwriting. And he was always hunting for deals. Garage sales, flea markets, you name it. He loved that stuff. He had a giant bowl next to the front door full of discount coupons."

"I think there was more paper in that bowl than in a copy of *War and Peace*."

The table laughed.

"He reused tea bags two or three times before throwing them out," said Jane, now smiling to herself, picturing her father in her head. "He'd turn off lights obsessively, never used the AC. He even added an on/off switch to his water heater so that it wasn't running all the time and wasting electricity. Though it *did* teach him to be good with his hands, didn't it?"

Mark nodded. "It sure did."

"Mr. Fix-It," said Jane. "He'd never take his car into the shop even when it was coughing out black smoke. He saw that as equivalent to setting a bag of money on fire. So instead, he'd just go to the library and borrow a car manual and teach himself how to fix the issue, whatever it was. And the issue would always get fixed."

"Absolutely. He fixed our riding mower. The vacuum cleaner. The garage door."

"The upstairs toilet."

"The upstairs toilet," repeated Mark.

"But he could just never relax," said Jane. "And it broke my heart. He was always, *always* worried about money. Always felt that wolf at the door. And it made him so unhappy. He just couldn't get over it. He became fixated on saving and accumulating and never letting anything go. Never spending a dime. I mean, he wouldn't even put his money in the bank—he was so against paying fees. He actually . . ."

Jane glanced around the table and looked again at Mark with a smile on her face. He smiled back, knowing what was coming.

"After he passed last year," said Jane, "Mark and I handled his affairs, selling off his few assets, cleaning out his home. As you might imagine, he was quite a hoarder. Why throw anything away if there was a chance at making a buck off of it somewhere down the road? Even if it *was* a snowball's chance in hell of being sold. But you should have seen his house. A rundown bungalow up in Pigeon Cove. Looked like some kind of survivalist's home. There were big plastic drums he'd used to catch rainwater that he'd then purify, a giant wood stove that he'd use as his heat source in the winters. He grew his own vegetables, had a number of chickens. He was hardcore."

"Rusted cars everywhere too," said Mark. "He'd fix them up or sell the metal for scrap."

"Needless to say, it took us some time to sort through all of that. And, well, we eventually got around to clearing out his refrigerator and . . ."

She laughed to herself and then looked around the table.

"And there was $200,000 inside."

A number of the league all looked at one another with expressions of complete incredulity on their faces.

"I think we'll take that one again," said Alan.

Mark and Jane laughed.

"Two hundred thousand," said Jane. "In cold hard cash."

"*Very* cold cash," said Mark.

"He wrapped stacks in Ziploc bags and kept them in his freezer. You should have seen our faces."

"Actually, we looked a little bit like you all do right now," said Mark, the table all chuckling.

"When was this?" said Alan.

"Last year," said Jane.

"Well, it sounds to me like you two have got your nest egg. How much is the boat?"

"A hundred grand," said Mark.

Alan smiled. "Buy the boat."

"I know. I know."

"But it's half your nest egg."

"But it's half our nest egg," said Jane. "Exactly. A big chunk of our financial future, as we see it. So we're having trouble pulling the trigger."

"I think we'd rather have the regret of not buying the boat," said Mark, "than not having the money down the road. Or at least that's what I tell myself."

"Yeah," said Jane, thinking about it. "Or maybe we're a couple steps away from putting the money in our freezer."

The table all laughed.

"Well, I've got good news," said Alan. "It's not terminal. It sounds to me like nothing more than a classic case of loss aversion."

Mark smiled. "It sure *feels* terminal."

"We all do it to some degree," said Alan. "No one likes to lose, period, but especially not money. And this can create a disproportionate amount of fear around investing, but it also affects your comfort level around spending. But you've got to strike the right balance. You've got to find the happy medium between enjoying your life now, today, while also making sure you'll be secure tomorrow.

"The thing about a loss aversion mindset is that it's only ever half the picture," continued Alan. "You only focus on the risks and not the potential rewards. You don't want to put your money into the market because the market's risky. And while it's true that there's always going to be risks, it's important to be clear-minded about those risks. But when you're dominated by a loss aversion mindset, you only focus on the market going down, only focus on losing, and so you think it's always going down, that you're always going to lose. Or that stocks going down is a purely negative thing. Remember: Down can be the best time to buy in. Now, how many people here are familiar with Maslow's hierarchy of needs?"

Alan glanced around the table and saw most of the league nodding their heads in affirmation.

"Well, Maslow's hierarchy provides a great template for how people should approach investing and spending," said Alan. "You want a foundation of liquidity for emergency situations, should anything go wrong. Cash for food, water, shelter, et cetera. But once that's been achieved, you can move on to your safety needs. Savings, investments, assets. And after that, you can start considering luxuries and dream purchases. You've now reached the boat stage."

The table all laughed.

"The problem is that a lot of people have trouble getting beyond that first level," said Alan. "They're constantly telling themselves that they're in emergency mode their entire life, even though by all accounts, they're secure. They have cash, they have savings, they have assets, and yet they're still worried that they're going to go broke next week, and so they do everything they can to avert that potential loss. Let me ask you something, if I may," he said, turning to Jane and Mark. "And let me know if I'm getting too personal. But is your mortgage paid off?"

"It is," said Jane.

"And you're both gainfully employed."

"We are," said Mark.

"And how much of that two hundred thousand have you spent so far?"

They both laughed.

"About as close to nothing as you can get without falling in," said Mark.

"How much of it have you invested?"

Mark and Jane looked at each other with sheepish smiles on their faces.

"Buy the boat," said Alan. "If nothing else, you'll transform some of that cold, hard cash into a tangible asset. But an asset that you two can enjoy for years and years to come. Life is not just about sacrifices, it is also about living a fulfilling life."

Jane and Mark turned back to the harbor and looked out over the water once more. The *Adventure* glided across the horizon in the distance like some intricate paper cut-out. A majestic vision of freedom and autonomy. The vessel both a relic from the past and a beacon of a brighter tomorrow.

They turned back to the others, and the table all smiled at them with expectant expressions upon their faces. A few of them glancing around at one another, their smiles widening. Then, as if it had indeed been rehearsed, they all turned back to the Darrows, and speaking completely in unison, the league exclaimed:

"*Buy the boat.*"

Chapter 6

OLD DOG, NEW TRICKS

THE LEAGUE sat enjoying coffee and dessert at their usual
table, having just finished a bold new feature the Beauport
Hotel chef was debuting. It was called Lobster Fra Diavolo,
a spicy dish consisting of lobster meat cooked in a garlic tomato
sauce with red pepper flakes and served over a bed of buttery
linguine. Needless to say, it was a hit, even among those who
were not accustomed to such heat, and indeed they were still
discussing it as their dessert was brought out: a creamy slice of
tiramisu that all the members savored with great satisfaction.
All but one.

"I've never had it," said Liz Stover.

"You've *never* had tiramisu?" said Gina.

Liz shook her head.

"You really have to try it," insisted Gina. "It's delicious."

"Thank you, but I'm really not interested," said Liz. "Something about combining chocolate and cheese just never seemed right to me."

The table laughed.

"Seems your portfolio isn't the only thing that needs diversification," said Alan, with a playful smile.

Liz laughed. "Oh, just you wait," she said. "I've a whole host of idiosyncrasies that you'll come to discover."

Alan smiled and glanced around the table. "Liz here is my newest client," he said. "We had our first meeting shortly before I formed our little Lobster League, so we're just getting to know one another."

"Well, perhaps the rest of us can get to know her as well," said Mark.

"Just what I was thinking," said Alan, turning back to Liz.

Liz took a look around the table and smiled. "I'm Elizabeth Stover," she said, "but everybody calls me Liz."

She had an austere face, now sixty-eight years old, and yet there was something very warm about her. A twinkle of sadness in her eyes made her seem more relatable. More human. As if her austerity were some sentinel protecting her inner feelings from getting out.

"I'm a piano teacher," she said. "Been playing my whole life."

"What do you like?" said Natalie, one musician to another.

"The classics," said Liz. "Chopin, Brahms."

"A woman after my own heart."

Liz laughed. "There were always classical records being played in the house when I was growing up," she said. "I had a very comfortable upbringing, as you might imagine. Upper-class parents. Upper-class grandparents, for that matter. Our family traces its lineage back to the early 1600s, when Captain Declan Stover, a master shipbuilder, helped establish Gloucester as a hub of the fishing industry. And the Stovers have been doing well ever since. We were in charge of one of the largest whaling fleets on the East Coast for a number of years. Doctors, servants, I believe there's even a couple of mayors in there."

Everyone chuckled.

"A part of the saltwater aristocracy," said Alan.

"Absolutely," said Liz. "I was brought up attending charity balls, sailing regattas, historical preservation fundraisers. My mother was a very proud woman, very elegant and refined, and she showed me the fine art of how to attend a gala. She studied baroque architecture in Europe and helped oversee the restoration of a number of Gloucester's historic buildings, so there was always a something-or-other to go to. My father was a Harvard graduate, a lawyer, and on the Maritime Museum board. He helped establish scholarships for the children of local fishermen."

"Sounds like you had a lot to live up to," said Jane.

Liz gave a smile. "I did," she said. "But if that's the price to pay for being brought up under such charmed circumstances, then I'd say I got off easy."

The table laughed.

"They were very protective, my parents," said Liz. "They basically arranged my marriage, setting me up on my first date with my husband. He came from good stock, they said. We married when I was twenty-six, the ceremony held at the Hammond Castle. A real blue-blood couple. Spencer worked for a white-shoe law firm in Boston—his father's—and so we lived very comfortably. Though I was often surprised we had *anything*, I later discovered just how much Spencer loved to spend. He just had a big appetite in general, always after the shiny new thing. He collected vintage automobiles. Ferraris, Porsches, old BMWs. Spent a fortune on clothing, luxury golf trips, lavish vacation properties. Though I suppose I took full advantage of those, so I can't really complain. Christmases in the Yucatan weren't so bad."

The group laughed.

"I would've liked to have children," continued Liz, "but . . ."

She trailed off, a silence overtaking the table.

"But I suppose it just wasn't meant to be," she said. "And Spencer didn't want to adopt. So that was that."

"How long have you been married?" asked Jane.

"We were together twenty years," said Liz. "Up until the moment I caught him in bed with two of my students."

A low gasp sounded from the group, a few throwing hands over their mouths, and all of them with stunned expressions on their faces.

"Yeah," said Liz, glancing around the table. "That's about the same look Spencer had on his face when I walked in."

The table chuckled, the tension now released.

"*Two* of your students?" said Natalie.

Liz nodded. "College girls," she said. "What can I say? I told you he had a big appetite."

More laughter.

"It was my fortieth birthday, the year I found out," said Liz, "and as a gift, he'd sent me and one of my girlfriends on a first-class trip to Vienna. It was a dream vacation. We took a boat cruise down the Danube, went to the state opera house. I thought it was one of the most thoughtful things Spencer had ever done. I'd been talking about going to Austria for so long. Well, little did I know that the trip was all just a plan to get me out of the house for a couple of weeks. While Spencer partied like he was Caligula."

Liz paused for a moment to take a sip of her coffee before continuing.

"I'd discover later that he just went wild while I was gone. And that he'd been going wild for quite some time. His midlife crisis, I suppose. Trading in his forties for two twenties. Anyway, I'd come to learn that he'd had countless affairs throughout our marriage, with law clerks, colleagues, even sometimes using escorts. Ladies of the evening, my mother called them. I really have no idea why Spencer did that. I mean, he was a very attractive man. He'd always had his pick of the litter. Oh well. The shiny new thing, I suppose."

Liz laughed to herself.

"Or maybe he really did just love spending that much," she said.

The group chuckled.

"But he was always flirtatious," said Liz. "From the day I met him. A player, a cad. I knew this before we even got together, his reputation preceding him, but I guess I just thought that I could change him. Or maybe I didn't. I don't know. Maybe deep down, I always knew what was going on, but I just turned a blind eye to it so that I could continue with the status quo. I think I felt special, to be honest, knowing that he could have anyone, but that he chose me. Sounds pretty vain, saying it out loud."

"Sounds human," said Alan.

Liz smiled warmly.

"Well," she said, "I'm sure you can guess by my upbringing what my parents thought about my getting divorced. They completely forbade it. I mean, my mother was Catholic, so she simply wouldn't have it. And I thought about staying. I thought long and hard about it. But I just . . . I just couldn't continue like that. Not after having discovered who Spencer really was with such unmistakable clarity. And the more I did think about it, the more I realized how dependent on him I'd become. How dependent I'd been on my parents before him. If I'd been dreaming of going to Vienna for so long, why didn't I just go? Why did I have to rely on Spencer to book the trip for me? We'd certainly enough money. And as I now know, Spencer certainly wouldn't have stopped me.

"But it all just made me realize I'd been completely conflict-avoidant my entire life. Completely dependent on others. It was rather juvenile, in a way. The girlfriend I mentioned, the one I took the trip with, she'd been married to a serial cheater herself and for even longer than I'd been. And she knew it too. And it never seemed to bother her. She just compartmentalized it, putting it out of her mind and never letting it pierce her perfect little bubble. But I saw how it ate away at her. I could tell. Like a flower slowly wilting, petal by petal. She's still married to the same man and—well, she's just a shell of her former self today. A Stepford wife or something. A perpetual smile on her face, and yet nothing behind it. And I love her, I really do—but seeing how she was, back then, I just knew I couldn't allow myself to live like that. Though I did wonder if I'd ever truly be able to break free myself."

"And did you?" asked Alan.

Liz nodded. "I got divorced."

"Good for you," said Natalie. "Hear, hear."

"I was determined," said Liz. "Though it was an incredibly anxious time for me. It was scary. And it caused a lot of friction between my parents and me. Between myself and some of my closest friends. Divorce was just something that was not done in our circle. You stuck it out, no matter how bad it got. But I did it. I filed, and it was a nightmare, but I hired a very respected family law attorney, and I did it. Though, boy, did Spencer drag his feet when it came to the settlement. Alimony, the division of assets. But eventually, I was set up, the settlement finalized, and I had more than I could ever need financially. It was then I began to further establish myself as the premier piano teacher in Gloucester too. I started making good money, soliciting wealthier clients, offering private house-call tutoring sessions. It was going well. Until it wasn't."

"Isn't that the way it goes?" said Rusty, nodding to himself. "The other shoe always falls."

"Well, about seven or eight years ago—and now this may sound strange," said Liz, "but I found a copy of *As I Lay Dying* by Faulkner in my basement. From a box of books that had been down there collecting dust ever since the divorce. I don't know how many of you have read the book, but it tells the story of a family's journey across the rural countryside on their way into town, carrying with them the casket of the mother. On the way, they encounter all sorts of trouble, but ultimately they arrive in town, and the father reveals—nearly immediately after the mother is buried, mind you—that they'd really taken this odyssey into town so that he could get remarried to a new bride.

"And as I'm staring at the cover, remembering the story, I flip to the first page, and there was Spencer's inscription to me. *With love.* It was a first edition. A Christmas present. And this would've been long after the affairs had begun. And it all just struck me with such brutal force. Did he know what he was doing in giving me that particular book? A book about a man burying his wife, a mother removed, to replace her with the shiny new thing? Maybe it wasn't intentional. Maybe it was just his subconscious trying to tell me something. Or maybe it was nothing at all. I mean, I love Faulkner. But for whatever reason, that feeling stuck with me. That feeling of being trapped both within a marriage and without.

"And it was then that I decided to modify our divorce settlement so that I would no longer receive alimony. I just felt it would be . . . disrespectful if I continued. I don't know how to explain it."

"Disrespectful to your husband?" said Alan.

"To myself," said Liz. "I might not have been married to him anymore, but I was still financially dependent on him. And I just couldn't abide that any longer. That clock had run out. I was earning from teaching piano, of course, but that paled in comparison to the support I was receiving. So I just cut it off completely. Though I did keep my share of our stock portfolio. That was mine. That had gone back for generations in my family, as it had in Spencer's. You see, both of our families made a fortune investing in AT&T and GE and a few other stocks of that nature. Blue chips. My grandparents had held them, my parents had held them, and so I held them too. It was just what was done.

"Anyway, things went well after that. I felt the freest I'd ever felt in my entire life. Completely on my own. Independent. And it felt wonderful. But then . . ."

She turned and looked at Rusty with a smile. "What always happens?" she said.

Rusty smiled. "The other shoe falls."

"Indeed," said Liz. "The penny drops. And in my case, rather literally. My piano work started to dry up considerably, students moving away, with fewer and fewer people interested in learning piano in general. I'd even started to develop a nasty bit of arthritis that hindered my playing."

She glanced down at her hands and rubbed one over the other.

"That was a real blow for me," she said. "I just couldn't play the way I used to. Which meant I couldn't teach the way I used to. So I started thinking of retirement, and that felt just about like falling off a cliff to me. I was Gloucester's favorite piano teacher, that's what I'd always been, since I was a young woman. So now, who was I? What do I do with myself? To potentially go from working to not working so quickly, to lose my only real source of income, was terrible. I'd still had my investments, but—this was just a couple years ago now—those had taken a turn for the worse too.

"The outlook on AT&T and GE had not been great for a while, but I had no idea. As I said, this is what my parents, my grandparents, had always done. But I'd quickly discover that my portfolio had gone from twenty million down to ten in relatively short order. And that was terrifying. It was catastrophic. I was quickly becoming unable to earn, and now my portfolio was in decline. It was a risk I didn't foresee or even think possible. So

I was having a full-blown identity crisis at this point. For most of my life, I'd identified as a piano player, as a wife, as wealthy, and now all these things were being stripped from me, and I had no idea how to handle it."

"So what'd you do?" said Natalie.

"Well, for one thing, I went to see Alan."

Alan gave a modest smile. "I'd no idea you were going through all that," he said. "You've got quite the stiff upper lip."

"Though apparently not here with the Lobster League," said Liz. The table laughed.

"Well, thank you for sharing," said Alan. "You know, they say you can't teach an old dog new tricks, but I'm not sure I buy that."

"No?" said Liz, a wry smile on her face. "Then go on. I'm listening."

"First, you diagnose the issue," said Alan. "Which I'd say in your case is nothing more than status quo bias. Just take a look at your portfolio. AT&T, GE. You invested in what you knew. Because it's what your family had done. And I think this is why you've encountered a personal identity crisis too, as you put it. Your identity has become intertwined with what you do, with all that you know: playing and teaching piano. You've developed a status quo bias with regard to yourself—or your view of yourself—in parallel with your investment strategy."

"So that's the diagnosis," said Liz. "And the treatment?"

Alan smiled. "Same as with your portfolio," he said. "Diversification. Or, better yet, think of it as a transition full of new and exciting options. Redefine your identity by exploring new interests, new avenues. You really shouldn't look at it as a crisis. It's a wonderful opportunity, and an opportunity that most people never get. You have the chance to discover who you really are, what you like, what you don't. Not what your husband liked, what your parents liked, but your own unique preferences. You said you focused on the classics as a piano teacher, right? Chopin, Brahms."

"That's right."

"Well, branch out," said Alan. "Why not add Schoenberg and Liszt too? What about twentieth-century music?"

Liz nodded to herself, considering the suggestion.

"A bit of Elton John, perhaps," said Alan. "Some Beatles."

Liz smiled. "Perhaps."

"Maybe some modern Top 40s."

"Now, now, let's not get crazy."

The table laughed.

"I imagine a lot of pop songs are much easier to play than the classics too, right?" said Alan. "So you might be able to manage despite the arthritis."

Liz nodded.

"And you mentioned a lot of your students have moved away," said Alan. "So why not go international yourself? Have you ever taught over the internet? On a Zoom call, for example?"

"I have not," said Liz.

"So then. Broaden your horizons beyond Gloucester. You can teach piano to anyone in the world. Increase your client list, your earnings. You could even rekindle your relationships with some of the old clients who moved away. Again, just look at what we've done with your portfolio. It's all about diversification. We've invested in a mix of stocks and bonds, in various markets, and that's turned things around for you, hasn't it?"

"It certainly has."

"So, try it in your personal life as well."

Liz smiled and thought about it for a moment. Her eyes alight with excitement, with future possibilities. She glanced around the table, some of the league yet finishing their dessert. Then she turned and called for the waiter.

"On second thought," she said, the waiter standing at attention, "I think I will have a piece of tiramisu."

The waiter nodded and went to place her order, and Liz glanced around at the others with a smile on her face.

"Why not?" she said. "You only live once."

Chapter 7
GOLDEN VISIONS

L OBSTER THERMIDOR was on the menu this week. Fresh meat baked in a rich, honey-hued cream sauce made of egg yolks, Dijon mustard, and white wine, served in the lobster shell with a toasted breadcrumb crust. The servers rounded the table and plated the dishes before all the members of the league, the entrée yet steaming, the aroma intoxicating.

David Flynn glanced over at his wife, Tracy, and smiled and gestured back to the lobster in front of him.

"Golden," he said, commenting on the color of the sauce, the crust.

Tracy laughed and shook her head before beginning her lunch with the others.

"What's golden?" said Alan.

"Oh, it's nothing," said David. "Tracy and I were just talking this morning about my *golden visions*, as she calls them. My attraction to the finer things in life."

"Attraction?" said Tracy. "More like obsession."

David laughed.

"There's nothing wrong with a little luxury, is there?" said Rusty, taking a bite of his lobster. "That's what it's there for."

"Even if you wind up in the poorhouse?" said Tracy with a smile.

"Well, now I think the floor is officially yours," joked Alan. The table all laughed.

"We've been having a little trouble with . . . home maintenance, shall we say," said David. "The finer things always seem to come with all sorts of hidden surprises, don't they?"

"We own the Breakers estate," said Tracy. "In Magnolia."

Rusty whistled sharply, very impressed.

"That's *yours*?" he said. "That place is a palace."

"Thank you," said David, a proud smile crossing his face.

Rusty looked around the table and filled the others in.

"You should see this place," he said. "It's a castle. Nine thousand square feet. A historic Tudor-style estate with its own caretaker's cottage. Wood-beamed ceilings, a granite oceanfront terrace. It's even got its own movie theater."

"Have you been moonlighting as a realtor, Rusty?" joked Alan. The group laughed.

"Never too late!" said Rusty, with a big smile on his face. "But, no, Marjorie and I went to an open house at the Breakers many years ago. What a house."

"A gorgeous place," said Marjorie. "You two should be very proud."

Rusty looked back at David. "You must be some kind of robber baron to afford that place."

"Some might say," David said. "I'm a cardiothoracic surgeon. At Massachusetts General."

"Wow," said Natalie Barnes. "I knew doctors were well-paid, but geez."

"Years ago, we made some smart real estate investments," said Tracy. "With Alan's guidance, of course. And they've borne significant fruit."

David's gaze drifted, and he smiled softly to himself, losing himself in a reverie.

"I'd wanted The Breakers ever since I was a teenager," he said. "I'd ride my bicycle past it, the ocean air on the breeze, the grackles and wrens sounding from the tall white oaks beyond the property fence. I'd daydream about what went on inside. What kind of parties, events, and backroom dealings were happening inside those walls, the VIPs who spent time there, wondering whether I'd one day become one myself. If I'd become important enough to *own* the Breakers."

"And here you are," said Alan.

"Here I am," said David.

He slowly emerged from his nostalgia and looked around the table.

"Obviously, you can see that Tracy's claims of my golden visions are completely unfounded," he said.

The group all laughed.

"But who knew gold could rust," said Tracy, offering a bittersweet smile. "You may be surprised, but owning a nine-thousand-square-foot mansion can come with one or two drawbacks."

"*The Drawbacks*?" said Rusty. "Were they the previous owners?"

The table laughed again.

"Go on," said Alan.

"Well . . .," said Tracy. "I was taught it was impolite to complain about your successes."

"Not here at the Lobster League," said Alan. "Not among friends."

"Well, maintenance and property taxes aside," said Tracy, "there're just so many extra expenses that we could have never foreseen. Call us naive, but landscaping, housekeeping, and, my God, the insurance? Turns out maintaining an oceanfront property in the Nor'easter Alley carries with it a large price tag."

"It was supposed to be an investment," said David. "An asset."

"And yet it's slowly turned into a liability. We're actually *losing* close to $100,000 a month on the home. We've tried to make it work—David had a few classic cars that we recently sold off, we had a vacation home in Clearwater that we got rid of—but it hasn't been enough."

"Though once the kitchen renovations are done, that should calm things down for a while."

"Until the guesthouse work starts in the fall," said Tracy. "And we've got the winterization, the weatherproofing after that."

David exhaled. "I know," he said. "I'm just trying to rationalize."

"Have you thought about downsizing further?" said Natalie. "Perhaps selling?"

"We have," said David. "But . . . I just can't do it."

"How come?" said Rusty. "Don't get me wrong, like I said, I've been to The Breakers—it's a dream house. But it is also *just* a house."

"Not to me it isn't," said David. "To me it's . . ."

He looked around the table, hesitant to continue.

"Friends among friends," said Alan.

David smiled thinly and continued.

"In my first year of med school," he said, "I was in a mentorship that partnered me with a fellow at Mass General, where I was introduced to Dr. Theodore Carmichael. *Teddy.* He was one of the leading thoracic surgeons in the country, a complete rock star, and for whatever reason, he took a shine to me. Showed me the ropes. And it eventually turned into one of the most profound relationships of my life. Because he didn't just train me on the technical aspects of being a doctor, but the social ones as well. How to deal with patients, how to deal with stress. With handling life-and-death decisions. Taught me how to schmooze the philanthropists at the fundraisers. He was an extremely gregarious person. Always the life of the party. Always holding court. A man who knew how to enjoy himself."

Tracy laughed. "Now that's an understatement."

"He knew how to spend," said David. "He'd a collection of vintage muscle cars, four houses, vacation spots. He even had this giant Fabergé egg, if you can believe it. I mean, it was utterly ridiculous, but he thought it was funny. He said that's what rich guys do. He had this 1968 Ford Mustang too. A GT 390 Fastback in Highland green. The exact same model Steven McQueen drove in *Bullitt*. I swear, my eyes nearly popped out of my head when I first saw it. I'd dreamed of owning that car since I saw it onscreen as a kid.

"Actually, I remember my freshman year in high school. I'd a crush on this girl, Teresa Whitmore, and the winter prom was coming up, so I decided I was going to ask her out. I was determined. I spent the night prior practicing what I was going to say in front of the bathroom mirror. And so the next day, I marched up to her, my legs like jelly beneath me, and just as I was working up the nerve to talk to her, everyone's heads turned toward the parking lot. Everyone's attention was stolen by the roar of a big-block V8 engine. It was Parker. Parker Van Houten. And he'd just pulled in his new Ford Mustang. It wasn't a '68, wasn't green, but still. It was a beast. And all he had to do was look out his window at Teresa and wave her over, and that was that. I mean, it was like something out of a movie. He cranked the Zeppelin up and flashed his million-dollar smile, and Teresa was his. And I think at that very moment it confirmed something for me."

"Confirmed what?" said Alan.

"That the Ford Mustang had magical powers. That it was capable of making your wildest dreams come true."

The table chuckled.

"It was actually Teddy who got me inside the Breakers for the first time," continued David. "It was unbelievable. He picked me up in his Mustang and took me to this cocktail gala the then-owners were having on behalf of some foundation. There were countless VIPs there. A couple film stars. They even got Sting to play a short set. You believe that? I'm watching him play *Fields of Gold* in the living room with fifty or sixty people. It was surreal. And not just to see all these impressive people in one room, but to see that kind of wealth on display. I mean, how much was Sting's fee alone?"

Laughter.

"And so to see Teddy moving through it all so effortlessly, to see how much respect and admiration was thrust upon him—well, it was hard not to envy him. And many years later, actually, it was

Teddy who introduced me to Tracy. I mean, he really did confirm everything I'd always thought when I was young."

"And what was that?" said Alan.

"That the wine tastes sweeter on Mount Olympus."

The table laughed.

"So years later, when I discovered the Breakers was up for sale," said David, "I just couldn't pass it up. Even if it was a bit out of our price range. But my practice was going well. And you have to understand that being able to own that house confirmed my success in a way nothing else could. Not to me. Owning it was not just a desire, but seemed more like the natural and correct order of things. Every great man had his great home, Teddy once told me. And even though Tracy and I have run into some issues . . . as long as we have the house . . ."

"Then you're successful," said Alan, finishing David's thought.

"Yeah. Something like that."

"I certainly didn't help things," said Tracy. "As soon as I saw that house, I fell in love with it too. How could you not? I'm no stranger to golden visions myself. I love the finer things as much as the next person. But sooner or later, it starts to slowly wear off, doesn't it? The thrill fades. And then it starts to feel like you're just keeping up with the Joneses. Chasing other people's dreams. Attaining all these expensive things just because that's what everyone else is doing."

David smiled. "Tracy would say, 'Instead of keeping up with the Joneses, why don't we just try to bring them down to our level?'"

More laughter. Yet David looked away, his face softening, growing more melancholic.

"I just . . . I'd never wanted anything like I wanted the Breakers," he said. "And now I have it. Or *had* it, I suppose."

"You sold it?" said Alan.

"Not yet, but . . ."

Tracy reached over and set her hand atop David's, the two of them exchanging a tender look for a moment.

"Now we find our *next* paradise," she said.

David nodded.

"At what point did you realize you might need a change, Tracy?" said Alan. "When was your own reality interrupted?"

Tracy shrugged. "When the bills started piling up," she said. "When I realized we were losing money on something that was supposed to be an asset. I just began to see that we were headed down a bad path. I mean, you have the house, and you have the reputation of owning the house, whatever status that brings—but you start to accept, however begrudgingly, that the house, the big-ticket item, may no longer represent to you what it did initially. It may not represent what you really value underneath. And I'm talking spiritually now, though of course it may also not represent the same financial value as well.

"But I'd say I started to grow really concerned when I realized that this one purchase, as lavish as it was, was starting to change who David and I were. Started to change our personalities, if only slightly. Wealth can skew your perspective if you're not careful. You start to believe in the illusion that 'Hey, I'm successful, I'm important, so I need to live in an important kind of house to demonstrate just how successful I really am.' And not just to demonstrate your success to yourself, but to confirm it to others as well."

David sighed and nodded slightly.

"They can get away from you, can't they?" he said. "Your values. As full throttle as Teddy was, even he himself warned me about this happening. He was a very self-aware man in a lot of ways, though that may not have been obvious to others. But he told me it was extremely common, with doctors especially, this kind of, I don't know what you'd call it—a narrow-mindedness. A sort of tunnel vision where you see only what you want to see. You reach a certain level of success, and you start to believe the hype. Start to believe in your own self-importance. So you buy the new house, the new car, all the material goods you can afford, and you're doing well, and people love you, so you keep down that path. You put the pedal to the floor. But eventually—and always much too late—you examine your cash flow and realize that you've gotten completely out of proportion. Your house, your expenses, they've become completely unmanageable.

"But by now, you've reached a ceiling. You're already making one or two million a year, so you can't really grow much more beyond that in terms of a salary. And so your net worth starts to dwindle. Yet even after you realize the score, you can't stop. Teddy himself has this problem. He just couldn't stop spending. It didn't matter that he was drowning in debt. And it ruined his marriage. It'll ruin a lot of marriages if you're not careful."

David glanced over at Tracy and squeezed her hand.

"My first marriage, I ran into this issue," said David. "We met while I was in med school, still on the upswing. I could see it coming, if I'm honest, the brick wall we were hurtling into, but I just couldn't stop. It was more, more, more. And, well, you get into some very bad, very hurtful habits when you're flying high. I mean, the clothes, the cars, the everything—it was a confirmation to me. They were totems of my success. All cards on the table, all the material toys were a strong source of personal self-worth in those days. Still are, I suppose. And so my first marriage crashed and burned hard. As did my second. But with Tracy, I just . . . I'm just not going to let that happen."

"And what changed for you, David?" said Alan. "And by the way, before you answer, it's very clear that your mentor wasn't the only one with some self-awareness. Both you two seem to have a firm grasp on your issues."

"Thank you," said Tracy.

"What changed?" said David.

He looked away, his face clenching tight with emotion. Tracy put her hand on his back and rubbed it slowly, and after a moment, David took a breath and looked back at Alan.

"Teddy passed away last week," he said.

The table all let out a sigh of great sympathy.

"I'm sorry for your loss," said Rusty. "Sounds like a rough one."

"Thank you," said David. "It was . . . we had a nice send-off for him. Had a large service for him and then a private one out on Eastern Point. We scattered his ashes in the ocean. I was surprised he lasted as long as he did, to be honest. He'd been a smoker his whole life, a heavy drinker. It's kind of ironic, though. A leading thoracic surgeon dying of heart failure.

"But what changed, what really did it for me and snapped me back to reality, was discovering that Teddy died broke," said David. "I always knew he was a spender, as I said, but he didn't even have anything saved away for the funeral. His nephews had to pay for everything. Seventy-three years old, and he had nothing to show for it. Nothing but debt. And I know way too many doctors, myself included, who are in the same boat. Living completely out of proportion. Their net worth next to zero because of their spending. And, well, with his passing, learning about the state of his finances, I just saw the writing on the wall in a way I never had before.

"Teddy burned through four marriages and had a fractured relationship with his children. And I just couldn't let that happen to me. When I was young, he was a god to me, but now, looking back, it just all seems so sad. He had some kind of emptiness inside of him that could not be filled, no matter how much money and cars and women he threw at it. I mean, it all starts to turn into a kind of insanity after a while. Repeating the same thing over and over again. But he was the top surgeon, he was king, he was *the guy*. And so it just confirmed all his choices and enforced his sense of self-importance. But fortunately for me it made me realize that I don't want to be that guy. Not anymore. And I realized I don't want to lose what matters to me most."

He took Tracy's hand in his again, and they shared a warm, loving look with one another.

"You two should be proud of yourselves," said Alan. "It takes guts to be honest with yourself. And to do so in front of a group of people. But I think you already know what you're supposed to do, don't you? Though perhaps I can shed some light onto *why* you've gotten into this specific predicament, if I may."

"Please," said David.

"It seems your whole life—even since the Ford Mustang, that jock in high school—you've associated success with material things," said Alan. "And then once you met Teddy, this very powerful and magnetic mentor who so clearly epitomized success to you, well, how could you resist? You saw this bright, electric person and said, 'Yes. Now *that's* what success looks like.'

"So it was confirmation bias. You associated success with certain material milestones, and owning the Breakers became the dominant one. Buying that house confirmed to you that all your actions leading up to that moment were correct, and so when the wheels started to come off financially, it was almost impossible for you to look at the house objectively. As a liability. It's obviously so much more to you than just an asset or even a home. As you said, it represents a source of self-worth for you.

"Now this is incredibly common—judging ourselves by what we have instead of who we are and then confirming our image of ourselves based on the possessions we own—but getting back to what Tracy said, wealth can distort our perceptions. But with enough time, enough distance, we can indeed look at our choices a little differently, and see that some of them were born out of incorrect assumptions. Namely, that having nice things makes you important or defines who you are. It was a non-negotiable for you to have a big house. And not just any house, but *that* house in particular. The Breakers. You had to have it. And then you got it. So now you're fully invested. Now the house represents a priceless possession, as there's so much of yourself wrapped up in it, and so even when it's clear it's a liability, how could you possibly walk away?"

David leaned his head back in a gesture of understanding. An a-ha moment for him.

"Owning the Breakers confirmed you were a success," said Alan. "And it seems, largely based on your mentor's intoxicating influence, that you became dead-set on maintaining that image of a successful person. And so, continuing to own the house became the number one priority in your life. The primary source of pride. But you need to redefine your definition of success. And I think you already have."

"I have?" said David.

"You both are putting the success of your marriage above everything else," said Alan. "And, if fully committed to, that in and of itself will relieve your financial stress, won't it? It will lead to you making the right financial decisions. Look, it's OK to grieve the loss of your home. Of any home. Some people may find it silly, but the Breakers is obviously very important to you. So grieve the loss. And then, hard as it might be, move on. If nothing else, it seems Teddy gave you a gift with his own reckless spending. He showed you the path to avoid. One final lesson passed down from mentor to protégé."

David nodded to himself, considering Alan's words. After a moment, he turned to his wife.

"I guess the only thing left is to start looking for our next paradise," he said.

Tracy smiled and nodded. "There's nothing wrong with having golden visions," she said. "So long as they fit in our budget."

David laughed and then looked around the table and grinned. In that moment, he seemed to arrive at some kind of acceptance, and he soon turned back to Tracy with a wide smile on his face.

"All right," he said. "We'll call the realtor tomorrow. On one condition."

Tracy smiled. "And what's that?"

"I'm keeping the Mustang."

Chapter 8
A TEAM SPORT

WITH A loud *crunch,* Rusty Jenkinson squeezed his cracker tight around the cherry-red lobster claw, exposing the delicious, steaming meat within.

"Hooo, there she is," he said.

The dish was traditionally prepared this week. Served with lemon, roasted asparagus, and a ramekin of warm drawn butter, the whole broiled lobster was split down the middle and brushed with garlic herb butter made from parsley, thyme, and smoked paprika. Breathing in the aroma, the group all dove in with their crackers cracking and their seafood picks picking.

Rusty wiped his greasy fingers on his lobster bib, dipped a large chunk of meat into his butter, and then took it down. He grinned with deep satisfaction at his wife, Marjorie, beside him, and she grinned right back.

"And they say money can't buy happiness," he said.

The table all laughed.

"I'd steal the meat off your plate," Rusty said to Marjorie, "if I weren't worried about appearing . . . *shell*fish."

A number around the table chuckled at the joke, a number more groaning playfully at the bad pun. Rusty then grabbed another lobster claw, wrapped his cracker around it, and, rotating his torso simultaneously, pantomimed cracking his back as he crunched into the lobster shell.

"Aaaahh, my chiropractor's been trying to work that out for weeks now," he said.

More laughter. Marjorie shook her head, smiling at her husband as she finished the last of her meal. "I can't take you anywhere," she said.

Rusty glanced over at Marjorie's brother, Mark Darrow. "What do you think, Mark?" he said, teasing his wife. "Think it's time your sister and I finally ended our charade and filed for the big D?"

Mark smiled. "You know, I did always think you were too good for her," he said, tongue-in-cheek.

"Quiet, you," said Marjorie, before turning back to Rusty. "And you never had it so good in your life."

Rusty smiled. "When you're right, you're right."

"So what do you do for work, Marjorie?" said Liz Stover.

"Rusty and I run our own HVAC company," said Marjorie. "Jenko Solutions. I'm the bookkeeper."

"'We care about your air,'" said Rusty, citing the company's slogan.

He'd finished with his meal as well and soon had the rest of the league. Their servers arrived to clear their lunchware and their finger bowls, offering coffee and dessert to the table. Rusty leaned back in his seat and patted his stomach.

"Boy-o, that was delicious," he said.

"So Rusty, what do you do at Jenko?" said Ed Farmer. "Installations?"

"Yessir. I was taught how to do HVAC in the service," he said. "US Army, First Infantry Division, during the Gulf War. As you can imagine, air conditioners were a prized commodity during Operation Desert Storm."

The group laughed.

"So when I got back," he continued, "I didn't really know what else to do. So I bought a truck and just kept on going with HVAC. Started my own business, met Marj, and the rest is ancient history."

"*Ancient?*" said Marjorie, in mock outrage.

Rusty gave a mischievous smile. "Come on, you know I'd be nothing without you," he said. "Certainly the business wouldn't be."

He turned to the group.

"I have zero acumen when it comes to the financial side of things," he said. "As I like to tell our clients: I'm the ductwork and she's the data. I'm in charge of cash flow and trash flow and nothing in between."

More laughter.

Rusty's phone then *dinged* upon the table with a text notification, and he retrieved it and put it in his pocket.

"Sorry about that," he said. "Bad table manners. Another thing my better half taught me."

"It's been a long road to domesticate him," said Marjorie, "but we're finally making some progress."

"So, Rusty," said Alan, "no interest at all in learning about the company's numbers? Never hurts to get the whole story."

"Don't confuse me with the facts," said Rusty, grinning. "I go out and make the money, and Marj makes sure it's still there by the end of the week. Being in the service taught me the value of divvying up responsibilities. The engineers clear the mines. The infantry clears the cities. The tanks clear everything else. Everyone has their role, and everyone matters, but it's none of my business knowing precisely what role the next guy plays. And I'm just not a numbers guy. Never have been. I'm a *feel* guy. I run on instincts."

"Even when your instincts tell you to purchase a rent-to-own sofa set at 200 percent APR," teased Marjorie.

Their servers returned, delivering coffee and cake to the league, and Rusty began pouring a healthy dose of cream into his coffee.

"Well, whatever comes our way, we always best it, don't we?" he said.

"That may have been true in the past," said Marjorie.

Rusty stirred his coffee with his spoon and glanced over at her. He saw now the seriousness on her face and grew sympathetic.

"What?" he said.

"I received a letter this morning," said Marjorie. "The Wilsons are suing us?"

"*What?*"

Rusty let out a frustrated exhalation and shook his head. He thought about things for a moment, sharing a quick glance with his brother-in-law Mark, before quickly reemerging as his old jovial self. He shrugged.

"Well, then I guess we'll see them in court," he said. "It'll give me a chance to wear that new suit that's been gathering so much dust in the closet."

"I don't know," said Marjorie. "It's . . ."

She hesitated, glancing at Rusty before glancing around the table.

"It's OK," said Rusty. "*They've* all shared with *us*."

Marjorie turned back to him and smiled flatly. "Well, they're claiming $70,000 in damages."

"*What?* No," said Rusty. "No, that's just ridiculous."

"A few weeks ago," said Marjorie, speaking to the league now, "we hired a subcontractor to install a unit in a young couple's home—the Wilsons. We were overbooked, so we went to this kid—some twenty-something-year-old who had been referred to Rusty by a colleague—and apparently he screwed up quite severely."

"Big time," said Rusty, nodding his head.

"Wound up causing significant water damage to the Wilson home."

"Though nowhere close to seventy grand."

"And this morning I received notice from the Wilsons that they're taking Jenko to court," said Marjorie, turning back to Rusty. "Our insurance premiums are going to go up."

"I know it."

"And who knows how it'll affect our reputation."

"Yeah."

"So maybe *now* you can start taking the financials seriously? You don't need to be a numbers guy to know this isn't good."

Rusty nodded. "No, you don't."

"That's rough," said Alan. "But, Marjorie, if I may—sometimes things that come naturally to us can be incredibly difficult for others to grasp. Financially or otherwise."

"Preach, brother," joked Rusty.

Alan laughed. "But that doesn't mean you shouldn't try," he said.

"Amen," said Marjorie.

"Simple things like just doing a basic will can even be difficult," said Alan. "This married couple I know, the wife wanted to draw up a will that would state who would take custody of their children if the guardians they already appointed passed away. Basically, who would be the fifth person in line. Well, the husband wouldn't even talk about it. And it's not that he didn't care. It's just that the minutiae of it all, to him, was so outside his wheelhouse that he couldn't concentrate. His wife tried to explain how important it was, if only to her, and the husband indeed tried to turn his mind to who this fifth person might be, but it just never got done. He just found it completely superfluous to worry about, and thus he never did. And it's simple things like that that can start to form cracks. One partner wants X done, but the other hardly sees the use, and so nothing gets done at all. It really just comes down to personality differences. To communication issues."

Rusty's phone dinged inside his pocket with another text notification, and he reached down and put the phone on silent and looked back at the group.

"Sorry again," he said. "I didn't realize I was so important."

The table laughed.

"But I hear what you're saying," he said to Alan. "I think in a lot of ways, Marj and I do see the world quite differently. She's corralling me to pay more attention to our personal finances, the finances of the business, and I'm constantly trying to explain to her what a British Thermal Unit is."

More laughter.

"But I think that's what makes us work so well," said Rusty. "What makes the company work. Our counter personalities leading to a stronger unit."

"But it *can* also lead to certain things never getting discussed," said Marjorie, pushing back. "It can lead to not vetting certain subcontractors."

Rusty glanced at her. A tense silence passed over the table.

"Marj, that's . . .," began Mark. "Go easy on him."

"It's all right," said Rusty. "She's right."

Marjorie looked from her brother to her husband and back again. She caught them both sharing glances, a look of conspiracy between them.

"What am I missing here?" she said.

Mark took another look at Rusty before letting out a deep exhalation.

"I was the one who recommended the kid to Rusty," he said. "The subcontractor."

"What?"

"He'd done a few jobs with me through Crescent Ridge, working on these new subdivisions of theirs, and he'd mentioned he'd done HVAC work before, that he was certified, so when Rusty told me he needed a guy, I gave him the kid's number."

Marjorie turned to her husband again, and he gave a flat smile.

"Rusty wanted to vet him first," said Mark, "but I talked him out of it."

"Why?" said Marjorie.

Mark shrugged. "Because he'd done such a good job previously. I thought he was genuine. But it was clear by what happened at the Wilsons' that he'd never done an AC installation in his life. Central or otherwise."

Rusty nodded. "The condensate drain line was installed sloping backward," he said. "The water was going nowhere but out over that basement floor."

"Why didn't you just tell me this?" said Marjorie.

"Because it got a lot worse," said Mark.

Marjorie turned back to her brother.

"When Rusty confronted the kid and learned that he was not in fact certified and that he'd lied to us," said Mark, "he said he wasn't going to pay him."

"I said I'd give him half," said Rusty. "And, well, the kid didn't take that too well."

He looked at his wife now.

"He stole one of our work vans," he said.

"Oh no, Rusty."

"Yes. And it was full of materials," said Rusty. "Refrigerant tubing rolls, copper line sets, condenser coils. In total, he made off with probably upward of sixty-five grand."

"*What?* Oh my God."

"I know. And I'm sorry for keeping this from you, but I just—"

"He did it for me, Marj," said Mark. "I was so unbelievably ashamed. I still am. It was bad enough the kid caused damage to the Wilsons' place, but then when he ripped off the van . . . Rusty was just protecting me. He *wanted* to tell you."

Marjorie regarded her brother for a long moment. Searching his face. A range of emotions flashing across her own. After some time, she looked back at Rusty.

"Is that true?" she said. "You were protecting him?"

Rusty nodded before shrugging. "Family is everything, right?"

Marjorie couldn't help but give a slight smile. She leaned back in her seat and thought about all that had been said.

"We need to call the police," she said.

"I have," said Rusty. "I've been speaking with a Detective Stahl, and he seems pretty confident that they'll catch up with the kid. It's pretty hard to just disappear nowadays. But I just wanted to sort this out with the kid and the van first, to know where we stood, and then address the Wilsons. I'd no intention of avoiding the issue."

"If we'd gone to see Andrea . . ."

"Marj, come on."

She glances at him with a playful, teasing look. She turns to the group.

"My girlfriend Andrea's a psychotherapist," she said.

"She's a quack."

"*Rusty*," said Marjorie. "She works with couples all the time."

"You really think we need that?" Rusty said earnestly. "We ain't perfect, but we're not half bad neither."

Marjorie reflected quietly for a moment. A thought arising in her head.

"You remember the Bensons?" she said. "Ran the flower shop over on Gage Avenue?"

Rusty simpered, nodding, knowing where she was going. Marjorie turned back to the group.

"This couple, Ron and Esther Benson," she said, "they were together forty years. Worked together, did everything together. This sweet, forever couple that seemed to really have the secret. On the outside, at least. Because it turns out that underneath it all, by the end, they were completely miserable. Year after year, they had drifted apart until one day the husband just left. Apparently, she told him she wasn't happy, that she wanted a divorce, and so he didn't even hesitate. He signed the papers and the next day rode off down to Acapulco. Never looked back. As if he'd been waiting for years for her to call it off."

"But are *you* miserable?" said Rusty.

"No," said Marjorie. "Not even close. I just . . . I don't want unspoken things between us becoming the termites eating away at our foundations."

Rusty nodded slightly in understanding.

"I'm sorry," he said. "I should have just told you."

"If I may?" said Alan.

"Please," said Marjorie.

"While it's certainly not my area of expertise, I do deal with couples all the time, and you two really don't appear to need professional counseling."

"Especially when we're getting it for free right here," joked Rusty.

Alan laughed. "You two clearly adore one another," he said, "but seem to simply be having a tough time communicating. You want the same things, but you just see the world quite differently from the other. You're coming at it from different angles."

Alan took a sip of his coffee before continuing.

"Marriage—especially one where you're working together professionally—is a team sport," he said. "And you both bring equal value to that team. Rusty, being great at offense, and you, Marjorie, at defense. But in order to maximize your game, if you'll allow me to drive this sports analogy completely into the ground, you need both those units to communicate effectively. The goal is the same—to win the game—but if your offense and defense aren't coordinated, they only get in each other's way."

"So what's the play then, Coach?" said Rusty.

The table all laughed, Alan included.

"First, you need to define the endgame," said Alan. "Which would be the direction and future of your company, Jenko. Marjorie, you're the defensive coordinator here, preserving the wealth, minimizing expenses, and Rusty is the offensive. Going out and doing the installations, dealing with clients firsthand. But you need to communicate your needs, your situations, and your ideas more effectively to one another. Rusty, you were proactive with contacting the police about the stolen van—good offense—but you failed to communicate this to Marjorie. Perhaps if you had, it would have allayed some of her concerns regarding the Wilson issue as she'd have known you were on top of it."

"I think it would have," said Marjorie.

"Now, with the theft of the van and this upcoming lawsuit," continued Alan, "you've definitely got some financial challenges in front of you, which will require the both of you to be firing on all cylinders. But you're a solid team. You can do it. On the defensive, you're going to need to tighten up spending, shore up funds for an attorney, replace the stolen materials, while on the offensive side, you're going to need to secure more clients, more lucrative contracts."

Alan turned to Mark.

"Perhaps I'm overstepping here," he said, "but, Mark, you mentioned Crescent Ridge recently began work on a new subdivision project?"

"That's right," said Mark.

"Well, do they have anyone in line already to do the HVAC work?"

A smile spread across Mark's face. He looked over at Rusty and Marjorie, the two of them smiling back.

"No, I don't believe they do," he said.

"So perhaps you pitch Jenko to them," said Alan. "Jenko Solutions will install all HVAC systems in the homes for a bulk discount."

Mark smiled. "Yes, perhaps I'll do just that."

Alan leaned back in his seat, reflecting on the issue.

"Couple dynamics can be tricky," he said. "Especially in the workplace. Often good, well-intentioned people just happen to be the polar opposite of their spouse in terms of how they approach problem-solving, how they communicate. So it takes a bit of fine-tuning from time to time."

"And Jane and I discussed this," interjected Mark, "and we want to assist with the damages at the Wilsons'. With the legal fees. I'm partly responsible for this mess, after all."

Marjorie smiled at her brother. "Thank you, Mark."

Rusty leaned over and put his arm around Marjorie.

"We'll get through all this," he said. "Our little flower shop is far from closing, you'll see."

Marjorie smiled. "And neither of us is fleeing to Acapulco?" she joked.

"You kidding?" said Rusty. "You know how easily I burn."

The table all laughed.

Just then, Rusty's phone began to buzz again from inside his pocket, now repeatedly, receiving an incoming call.

"Don't stand on ceremony," said Alan. "Therapy session's over."

Rusty smiled and retrieved his phone from his pocket. Yet glancing at the call display, his face became serious. He looked over at Marjorie.

"It's Detective Stahl," he said.

He answered the call.

"Hello? Yes, hi, Detective."

He listened for a moment while the detective spoke.

"OK . . . OK . . ."

He listened further.

"Yes. Yes, absolutely. Thank you. I'll do just that. Bye."

He hung up the phone and glanced around the table. He'd a mercurial look upon his face that, very slowly, began to turn into a satisfied grin. After a moment, he looked back at Marjorie.

"They found the van."

Chapter 9
LOST AT SEA

IT WAS a gray afternoon when the group gathered the following week. A matte sky the color of steel, black storm clouds rolling in from the west, and though it was yet rather warm, the league decided to lunch inside for fear of rain. They sat in the corner of the dining room next to the windows and for the lamplights glowing amber and the earth-toned upholstery, and for the bonhomie that the group had established over the last two months, it was a cozy and congenial assembly despite the bleak-looking sky beyond.

They dined on lobster scampi. Tender chunks of lobster tail sautéed in garlic, shallots, and a healthy splash of sauvignon blanc, served over a bed of buttery linguine. Phil Barton sat finishing the last of his, enjoying his meal, and yet he could not stop glancing out the window as he ate. Looking out over the harbor. Looking toward the ocean.

He was a patrician-looking man, in his seventies, though still quite handsome. Distinguished with wizened eyes and a disarming smile. Something tender about his face. Something tragic. He dressed in a navy blazer over a merino-wool pullover and chinos, and though there was nothing flashy about his dress, for the cut and quality of the fabrics, for the aristocratic aura about him, he indeed gave the impression that he was a man of considerable wealth.

"What's out there, Phil?" said Alan. "Did you spot the Kraken?"

Phil turned and smiled before glancing back out the window.

"There's a topsail schooner out on the water," he said. "Way out there. Not a smart idea in this weather."

"How'd you spot that?" said Natalie, squinting her eyes, trying to see the tiny ship out in the distance.

"I suppose it's an occupational hazard," said Phil. "To uncover the unseen."

"Well, don't leave us hanging," joked Rusty.

Phil smiled. "I'm a judge," he said. "Well, retired. Superior Court. Worked a number of high-profile cases over the years. Louise Woodward, Whitey Bulger . . ."

"*Whitey Bulger?*"

"Yes, sir."

"Well done."

"And not a bad retail investor on the side," said Alan, smirking at him.

Phil shrugged. "I'm a tinkerer, that's for sure," he said to the table. "Much to the politely masked frustrations of my financial advisor here."

The group all laughed.

"What can I say," continued Phil. "I'll read something in the paper about this or that and call Alan up and say we need to sell this and buy that and move things in this direction. And then Alan spends the second half of the conversation trying to talk me down."

Alan smiled.

Phil turned back to the ocean. The distant ship just a tiny black pinprick on the horizon. His expression grew sad. Melancholic.

"My grandson, he . . ."

His voice trailed off. After a moment, he turned back to the table.

"My daughter—last week she sent me a drawing that my grandson Patrick had made," he said. "Showed his mommy and two older brothers at the bayfront, all smiling and happy, sun shining. And then, very small in the background, a small ship with a tiny person on it. He told his mother that it was Papa out there on the ship. Me. And when she asked why Papa wasn't on the shore with the rest of the family, Patrick said that it was because Papa likes being alone. That Papa doesn't like playing with us."

A collective sigh passed around the group. Phil gave a flat smile.

"Things have been a little strained with my daughter and me for a while now," he said. "She can be quite difficult sometimes. Hard-headed. Stubborn."

He thought about it for a moment. He relented. A moment of self-awareness.

"But then again, I suppose she does get it from me. I mean, her mother? A saint."

"Can you fix it?" asked Natalie, sitting beside him.

"I don't know. I mean, it's just life. We're just different people, Sammy and I. And it's just the order of things. You work enough criminal cases, you start to have your eyes opened."

"What *order*?"

Phil shrugged. "Atrophy, I suppose. All things passing away. It's a sad fact of life, but that doesn't change the fact. But listen, I don't want to bring the whole table down here. I'll leave that to the weather."

Laughter.

"You don't need to make excuses for yourself," said Natalie. "This is what we're here for. Warts and all."

"Well," said Phil, "I suppose the real trouble between Sammy and me started about a year or so ago. She came to me asking for money."

A few knowing groans let out around the table.

"That's always tough," said Ed. "Family asking for money."

"Thank you," said Phil. "Well, she wants to open her own restaurant and needs a fair amount of capital to get started. And look, she's a single mother with three boys, so I understand money's tight, that she can't do it on her own, but . . . most businesses fail within the first year, right? Another sad fact of life. And I didn't want that happening to her. Her failing. She's a very sensitive woman. Not to mention her being unable to pay me back when she goes bust. And that would cause a lot of stress and animosity between us."

"How much was she asking for?" said Alan.

"Ninety thousand."

"Oof."

"Yeah."

"That's a lot."

"So you foresaw it causing a rift between you two?" said Natalie. "You were trying to protect against that?"

"Exactly. But all Sam could focus on was me turning her down. I was just another bank declining her request. So she was very upset. She called me selfish, you believe that? She's got her hand out asking for money, and she's criticizing me? Well. That set us off down a bad path. We got into this huge argument, and things haven't been the same since. I'm showing up for the kids, birthdays, holidays, things like that—I mean, I'm *trying* to—but we're seeing each other much less than we used to. And you can just feel it. An icy vibe whenever we're together.

"But you see what I mean. I actively tried to protect against us falling out, and it happened all the same. This is what I'm talking about. Atrophy. It's just the way the wind blows sometimes. Most times, really. And ninety thousand dollars? That's a lot. And who doesn't worry about money? I'm in a good situation, but life happens. A couple bad breaks and you're lining up in the bread line. It keeps me up at night. The thought of destitution."

He glanced out the window again before turning back to the group.

"Rainy day funds are important," he said, offering a weak smile. "And I've sacrificed. Who hasn't? I've always wanted to do one of those *Titanic* wreckage deep-sea dives, for example. And I can afford it. On paper. But it's always the same tune. You go off and you have your fun, and then when you least expect it, you find out that the money you just spent is now completely vital. And you're standing there holding the bag."

"You can afford a *Titanic* voyage?" said Rusty. "Sheesh. Those things are like a quarter million a pop. Just how much money do you have, Your Honor?"

The table laughed.

"My financial advisor might know the exact figure," said Phil, looking to Alan.

Alan looked at him and glanced around the table before looking back to Phil.

"With your permission?" he said.

"You have it."

Alan turned back to the group. "All in, Phil's net worth is somewhere just north of a hundred million."

A collective gasp passed around the table. An audible shock.

"With a guaranteed lifetime pension of three hundred thousand a year," continued Alan, "and over a million from dividends and interest."

A silence grew. A judgment.

"I must say, it *does* sound silly, you being so worried about money," said Natalie, finally breaking the tension. "I really don't think you need to worry about the bread line."

Several of the league laughed, and Phil gave a smile and then looked to the window, a light drizzle now speckling the pane. Soon, they heard the pleasant sound of rain pattering down upon the deck outside.

"I'm aware it's slightly irrational," he said. "My money concerns. But . . ."

He turned back to the group.

"Everything goes away in the end. Doesn't it?"

He'd a great sadness in his eyes now. An overwhelming expression of loss, wounded and helpless. Natalie looked over at him with sympathy, with tenderness, and she soon reached out and set her hand over his and said nothing beyond that. Indeed, there was nothing more that needed to be said.

Phil looked at her with an expression of deep gratitude on his face. It seemed to help him hold it together, and he collected himself and looked back at the group.

"At a dinner many years ago," he said, "a friend of mine, a psychiatrist, he said I had a deep-rooted fear of abandonment. I hadn't asked for his diagnosis, by the way, but I accepted it nonetheless. At the rates he charged, I knew I was getting for free what his clients paid handsomely for. But this didn't come as any kind of shock to me. My father . . ."

Phil took a moment before continuing on.

"My father died when I was very little. When I was ten years old. He was a member of the Church of Christ, Scientist. His whole side of the family was. I think he was even a distant relative of Mary Baker Eddy, I recall someone telling me. Anyway, adhering to his beliefs, he avoided medical treatment his whole life. Which wasn't the worst thing in the world when I was growing up. No doctors, no check-ups. I mean, imagine telling a kid that he *never* has to go to the dentist? But then my old man got sick. And that was a different story altogether. You see, it was his belief—his faith—that illness was fundamentally spiritual in nature. That prayer was the only true medicine. And he wouldn't hear of anything else. You can see now where my daughter and I get our stubbornness from."

Polite laughter.

"So from then on, I always knew life was going to be short," he said. "Or that it certainly *could* be short. That the potential was always there. And then, ten years ago now, when I lost my wife, well . . ."

"My God," said Natalie. "You poor man."

"She had leukemia. And it was a very long and painful decline. It was awful. Well, after that, I was just completely lost. I threw myself into work and just tried to move past it. Tried to forget about it, really. Sam tried to get me to talk to someone, but I just couldn't do it. I could barely talk to *Sam*. I just kept on seeing my wife's face every time I looked at her. I suppose, thinking about it now, that's when the trouble between us really started."

A rumble of thunder sounded from outside. The rain falling heavier. A charcoal sky.

"Is that when you retired?" said Natalie.

"That was only a few years ago now," said Phil. "Though it's just semi-retirement. I still work occasionally."

"You're *still* working?" said Rusty.

Phil nodded. "I've reached senior status as a judge, so I maintain a reduced caseload," he said. "But, yes, I still sit."

"So you're still earning."

"Yes. Senior-status judges receive their full salary for life."

"And the salary? If I may be so bold."

"A quarter million," said Phil.

Rusty whistled sharply.

"And you *still* worry about money?" said Natalie.

Phil laughed to himself. A stifled, ironic laugh. Conscious of his irrationality. He turned to the window once more, looking out toward the horizon. The water choppy and dark. Whitecaps forming. He couldn't see the ship any longer.

"I just want my family to be taken care of," he said. "For them to be happy and secure, for when the big storm comes rolling in, whenever and *what*ever that may be. Because it *is* coming."

He turned back to the group.

"I'd like my grandson to start drawing pictures of me on land again," he said with a melancholy smile. "I'd like to see more of my family. That's what I'd like."

"I think you're much closer to that than you think," said Alan.

"Yeah?"

"Absolutely. From what I'm hearing, I really don't think it's as bad as you imagine. You're just seeing things through a certain perspective right now. Interpreting information through the lens of your preexisting narrative."

"What narrative?"

"Namely, that life is some tragedy just waiting to happen. And it's completely understandable—with your background, your experiences—it's clear why you'd feel that way. Your father passing away when you were so young and then your wife—how else could you feel about the world but pessimistic? And this has bled into your financial decisions. You're *looking* for problems where potentially none exist at all. Trying to find patterns in the news cycle that confirm your negative narrative bias."

"But . . . why would I do that?"

"Because although it may be negative, negative is familiar to you. It's what you've known. And so when it's validated, it's comforting, as paradoxical as that may sound. But it may have nothing at all to do with your actual reality. Correlation does not equal causation. Think about it. The stock market was down in 2000, in 2008, and so, therefore, people believed there *must* be some giant recession coming. And yet it didn't. It's always smart to plan for a rainy day, of course, but it can be equally as smart to plan for the sun. The other shoe doesn't always fall.

"You need to create new patterns," continued Alan. "A new story of the world and its constituents. You want your family to be taken care of, right?"

"Of course."

"But they already are. Financially, at least. Together, you and I have set up a trust for all three of your grandchildren, right? A college fund."

"Right."

"You've already taken care of your will. Your entire fortune to be handed down to your daughter and her children."

"Yeah."

"And you yourself are more than taken care of. I mean, forget about your investments—at the absolute minimum, your salary guarantees you a quarter million a year. So even if the mother of all unforeseen storms comes along, you're safe. Completely."

Phil nodded to himself.

"And if I might suggest something?" said Alan.

"Let's have it."

"Give your daughter the ninety thousand for her restaurant. At the end of the day, it's less than one-tenth of one percent of your fortune. So if her business doesn't work out, there's no harm to anyone. Financially, it'll be a blip on your balance sheet. Just give it to her as a gift and forget about it. I imagine it would go a long way with patching things up between you two."

"Yeah. You're probably right."

"You'll make her happy, you can see your grandkids again, and, as a gift, that's ninety thousand less from your taxable estate."

Phil smiled. "See, now this is why you're my financial advisor," he said.

The group all laughed.

"And if I might suggest something too?" said Rusty.

The table all looked at him, Phil included.

"Go on," said Phil.

"Take that *Titanic* voyage," he said, "if for nothing else than it will allow me to live vicariously through you. Just don't take an OceanGate submarine."

A spell of laughter around the table.

"Or better yet, just take me with you," continued Rusty. "C'mon, you can afford it!"

Phil laughed and smiled and glanced around the table, a look of gratitude settling on his face.

"You see?" said Alan. "There's always a silver lining if you wait long enough. Our lives are shaped by the stories we tell ourselves, so you better be careful about exactly which story you're telling. There are so many beautiful, positive things we can focus on beyond the negative. And even more so for a man in your position, a man with your means. So take the trip, call your daughter, and come back to shore with your family."

"I know," he said. "You're right. But it's just—"

He stopped himself. Another ironic expression.

"I'm doing it again," he said with a smile. "Walking the same path."

"Old ways of thinking can be very difficult to shake off," said Alan.

"No kidding. It's like fighting an undertow."

"Well," said Alan, now speaking to the collective, "welcome to decision-making and biases."

Chapter 10
MAD MONEY

THE LEAGUE casually eyed the Hurricane II vessel as it departed Gloucester Harbor, setting off on another Cape Ann Whale Watch tour. It was a majestic ship, a hundred and fifteen feet long, accommodating over a hundred passengers, and able to cruise at speeds of up to thirty knots. They watched it glide south as they ate, smooth and steady over the calm waters, nothing but sunshine and blue skies on the horizon, and soon it had cleared the breakwater, the Dog Bar Lighthouse, to begin its journey east toward that open sea.

They dined on Lobster popovers this week. Mouth-watering lobster meat sautéed with garlic, shallots, and herbs, and served inside a crispy, buttery roll made from a flour-egg batter. Flaky and airy, the golden popovers were plated three apiece and coupled with a crisp arugula salad. Cherry tomatoes, red onions, and all tossed in a lemon-honey vinaigrette, the peppery salad pairing perfectly with their savory main.

"Oh, before we forget," said Tammy Thurman, sitting with her husband Fred, "we're throwing a gala at the Cruiseport at the end of the month. And you're all more than welcome. I've got the invitations in the car, so come see me after lunch if you're interested."

"What kind of gala?" said Ed Farmer.

"It's a fundraiser for our son's new venture," said Fred.

"He and his college roommate developed a new digital something or other," said Tammy. "Some new app that . . . what does it do again?"

Fred smiled. "It uses AI technology to translate plainspoken speech into technically accurate programming code. So, people with little to no coding experience can create various computer systems. Software, websites, other apps. Things like that."

"But don't worry. You're not obligated to come," said Tammy. "I don't want this to feel like a shakedown or something."

The table all laughed.

Tammy and Fred Thurman were a handsome couple, in their late fifties, both fit and attractive. Tammy, with a lithe and toned figure, a result of her daily Pilates regimen, was dressed fashionably in a chic cashmere sweater over a silk charmeuse blouse and high-waisted trousers. She had a warm and pleasant demeanor with a girl-next-door smile. Fred, on the other hand, had a deep tan, thick silver hair, with something vaguely European about his dress sense. A slim-fitting, open-collar suit, sleek and sharp, with his silk dress shirt unbuttoned to a confident depth. On his wrist, an elegant Omega Seamaster watch.

Phil Barton sat beside them, and he glanced at the watch. "That's a hell of a timepiece you got there, Fred," he said.

Fred glanced at the watch himself. "Thanks," he said with a smile.

He looked to his wife, and she flashed him a playful, mischievous look.

"We did a little splurging the other week," she said to the table.

She collected her handbag and held it up. It was a classic maxi Chanel.

"We came into a bit of extra capital," she said.

"Sounds like your son doesn't need a fundraiser at all," said Rusty.

Fred laughed. "Oh, nothing like that kind of money," he said. "Just a bit of a windfall last weekend."

"Well, do tell."

Fred glanced at Tammy, seeking permission, and she shrugged. "Why not?" she said. "What happens at the Beauport, stays at the Beauport."

Fred smiled and turned back to the table.

"Tammy and I know how to count cards," he said.

A silence rose for a moment. A few league members glancing at one another, some shocked, others delightfully intrigued.

"*Really?*" said Susan Farmer. "That's so . . ."

"Badass," said Rusty.

Fred laughed and glanced over at Phil beside him. "Sorry, Your Honor," he said.

Phil shrugged. "Counting cards ain't illegal. Shoot, wish I knew how to do it myself."

"When did that all start?" said Alan.

"When I was at Dartmouth," said Fred. "Before Tammy and I even met. I came across a book that taught you how to do it, and so I just started testing it out. A few of the fraternities would host casino nights once a month, and so it was the perfect proving ground. Nothing like a bunch of drunken frat boys to use as guinea pigs. And I got pretty good at it. So I started expanding. I can remember the first time I walked into a casino—an actual casino—to test it out. I was so nervous. I was shaking. But I did well. Made a few hundred bucks, and that was good enough for me. I collected my chips and got the hell out of there."

The table laughed.

"And then after college," said Fred, "I just kind of forgot about it. I think I just chalked it up to another juvenile thing left behind. Like keg parties and togas."

"Speak for yourself," said Rusty.

More laughter.

"And then what happened?" said Alan.

"Then he met me," said Tammy with a smile.

"Not long after we got married," said Fred, "I told her I could count—I forget how it came up—and you should've seen her eyes light up. Like a flower blooming in time-lapse."

Tammy laughed. "And I got him to teach me how to do it," she said.

"It was exciting. The two of us in this . . . conspiracy with one another. It felt like we were Bonnie and Clyde."

"Let's hope it ends a little better for you two," said Phil.

Laughter.

"It spiced up the marriage, that's for sure," said Tammy. "Not that it needed spicing. But it just added this extra exhilarating element. I remember one long weekend we took a trip down to Atlantic City, and it felt like we were in the movies. It just felt so glamorous and dangerous and sexy. Even when things weren't going well."

She turned to her husband. "Remember them taking us to the backroom at the Tropicana?"

"How could I forget?" he said. "Thought we were going to lose more than our winnings."

"You got caught?" said Natalie.

Fred nodded. "That was the last time we played at the same table."

"And by then, we'd started going to Vegas," said Tammy. "I remember, when Fred surprised me with our first trip, I could've flown us both there on my back. I was so excited. Talk about glamorous."

"And you still go?" said Alan.

"Oh yeah. Around six or seven times a year, I'd say."

"Whenever we get the itch, really," said Fred.

"Yeah. The itch for a new handbag," said Tammy.

Fred laughed. "Or when there's nothing good on TV."

"But we're more disciplined with it now. We just play black-jack, separate tables, separate casinos, and each caps our earnings at five thousand a trip. Keep it small-time. It's just our bit of fun. Our mad money. We get the hotel comps, the free drinks, the free tickets, and have a great weekend."

"Ten grand a trip ain't so small," said Rusty.

Tammy smiled. "Well, perhaps not. But we're pouring it right back into the economy. It's our ritual. The day following our big night out, we always go shopping. Buy a new handbag, a watch.

Treat ourselves to high-roller dinners. Things like that. It's all just a bit of naughty fun, really."

"How long have you been doing this?" asked Susan.

"Started shortly after we got married," said Fred. "So over twenty years now."

"And it's still just as exciting," said Tammy. "Something to look forward to."

"Besides, we're both accountants. Have our own firm, Veritas Financial. So we've got a handle on things. We make sure to only go to places where they use two-card decks instead of four. Things like that. We never let it get out of hand. Five thousand each, that's it. Five thousand and then cash-out time."

"So is learning to count cards one of Veritas' financial planning strategies?" said Alan, tongue-in-cheek.

Fred and Tammy laughed.

"What accounting firms really need is an advisory service warning against ambitious children," joked Tammy, looking to her husband.

"No kidding," said Fred, before filling in the rest of the group. "We promised our son Brad—he's the one with the startup, our oldest—we told him that if he could attract three hundred thousand in capital from angel investors for his app, we'd match it. It was supposed to just be a bit of motivational rhetoric."

"You didn't think he'd actually do it?" said Alan.

"Bradley was always a bit shiftless growing up," said Tammy.

"A *bit*?" joked Fred.

"But he really came into his own in college. I don't know what got into him, but he was suddenly very motivated."

"I guess our bit of rhetoric worked."

"Up at four in the morning, working away. He and a couple of his college roommates."

"I don't know where he gets it from. Only thing I did in college was learn how to count."

Tammy laughed. "But now it's paying off for him," she said.

"Well, good for him," said Alan.

"Yeah," said Fred. "Only now we've got to pay up. We're expected to hand the money over at the fundraiser next week. There'll be a lot of VIPs there, apparently. He's invited several tech entrepreneurs, tastemakers, industry insiders. So he figures if we start the night off with a glossy photo-op of us handing over a giant check, that'll oil the gears for the rest of the guests."

"But you don't have it?" Alan said delicately.

"No, we do," said Tammy. "It's just . . ."

"It's a lot of money."

"It's a lot of money. Exactly."

"Even if we didn't have it," said Fred, "we'd find a way to raise it. Brad's already announced it and we'd never embarrass him like that."

"Not *that* badly, anyway," said Tammy with a smile.

"I wonder how he's going to take it when we reveal that the money's coming straight out of his inheritance?" joked Fred.

"I swear this all started when we started giving them gift cards as kids. Now he and his brothers just expect free money all the time."

"We've tried to instill in them the value of a dollar, but it's difficult. All they've ever known is wealth. All they've ever seen is valets and first-class cabins."

"But that's not how you and Tammy grew up?" asked Phil.

"Not at all," said Fred. "We both grew up working class. I was raised by a single mother. She worked as a hotel porter in the day and then moonlighted as a waitress at an all-night diner. I don't know how she did it. So it was always hand-to-mouth growing up. Not that I knew any different. I was born and raised in Roxbury in Boston. So everyone was struggling, especially back then. I mean, all my schoolmates were in the same position as me. It was just how it was."

"And yet you made it all the way to Dartmouth," said Alan.

Fred shrugged. "God bless the Stamps Scholars Program," he said. "Gave me a full ride."

"God bless your mother for forcing you to hit the books," said Tammy.

"And what about you, Tammy?" said Alan. "Same thing?"

"I had it a little easier," she said. "I grew up just outside of Albany. My mom was a cashier, and my dad owned a laundromat. So we never had much, but it was enough. Like Freddy said, when you're that age, you don't know any different. It's only as you look back as an adult that you realize just how much your parents sacrificed for you. How much stress they must've been under. But I made out. Worked two jobs to put myself through college, met Freddy, and together we built our accounting firm from the ground up."

"And why accounting?" said Phil.

Tammy smiled. "I guess we both like numbers."

"But we're very protective of the firm," said Fred. "Of what we've earned. It's like our fourth child. So cutting our son a three-hundred-thousand-dollar check . . . it's just a bit of a hard swallow."

"God help us when his brothers start coming to collect their own small fortunes."

"I think at that point we may indeed have to take up Bonnie and Clyde's profession," joked Fred.

Alan smiled. "People are much more protective of wins that are hard-earned," he said. "We always place a much higher value on the things that we've built ourselves. They call it the IKEA effect."

The table laughed.

"Doesn't matter if it's built of cheap wood and put together with an Allen key," said Alan. "*You* made it. You put it together. And so it means something to you."

"If you can get through constructing the damn thing without smashing it all to pieces," said Rusty.

Alan laughed before turning to the Thurmans again.

"I think what you two might really want to keep an eye on is the *endowment* effect," he said. "The flip side of the IKEA effect."

"The endowment effect," said Tammy.

"It's a bias that allows us to spend freely with money we feel we *didn't* earn," said Alan. "When we feel it's pennies from heaven and not money we worked for, we tend to treat it a lot differently."

"You mean, for example, by blowing it on handbags and watches?" Fred smiled.

"Exactly. The big one is inheritance. Research shows that people treat inheritance like lottery winnings. Like free money. And so people just go out and spend it. Blow it all on frivolous things and usually in short order. Even substantial amounts of money. It's very common. It doesn't make logical sense—a dollar is a dollar—but for some reason, if you win ten grand counting cards, for example, you just can't help but view that money differently than, say, if you were awarded an annual bonus of the same amount. The human brain just doesn't seem built to process the concept of free money.

"Look at young athletes," continued Alan. "Or musicians, entertainers. Anyone who accumulates money quickly. One of the most fascinating books I ever read was by this author named Steve Chandler called *17 Lies That Are Holding You Back and the Truth That Will Set You Free*. In the book, he discusses what a total disaster winning the lottery can be. It's like some cursed monkey's paw or something. Truly. Many people just get over-confident, and their spending gets away from them, and they wind up bankrupt. If you Google lottery-winning stories, it's just overwhelming the number of them that end in catastrophe.

"And in the book, Chandler compares several lottery winners, surveying them the year following their big win—and it's just a complete mess across the board. Either they blew all the money or they had to move out of town because all their neighbors hated them, were jealous, made them feel unwelcome. The grocer would no longer give a free cookie to their little girl because she was a millionaire. Or there's the calls out of the blue from the cousin or Uncle Eddie or some guy from high school asking you for fifteen thousand for his daughter's operation. And so their lives just became destroyed. They're euphoric initially, and then a year later, they're in crisis.

"But what Chandler did that was so fascinating to me, he also surveyed individuals who'd actually lost limbs. And it turns out that, though these individuals were devastated and miserable when they were first injured, a year later, they were even more grateful than they'd been *before* their injury. They were happier. And Chandler's conclusion was that people who lose a limb are typically much happier than people who win the lottery, as hard as that is to believe."

"Wow," said Rusty. "That's wild."

"You'd think if you fell into that kind of money," said Ed Farmer, "a hundred million, say, that you'd hire smart people to surround yourself with. Money people to advise you."

"The problem is you're not qualified to hire those people," said Alan. "You don't know what you don't know. *Why hire a financial advisor?* they say to themselves. *I'm already rich.* And then Uncle Eddie ends up being their only source of information on how to manage money, and all he does is confirm everything that they think they should do."

Alan looked back at the Thurmans.

"You mentioned giving your boys gift cards," he said.

"Easier than trying to pick out a gift," joked Fred.

"But—and everybody does this, so don't feel like I'm picking on you—but when we give our kids cash and gift cards, any kind of free money, that's how they're interpreting it. And then what's the first thing they're asked after they get the money? *What are you going to spend it on?* So there's this immediate association between getting money and spending it. I've often wondered if this type of association leads young people to problems when they first receive credit cards."

"I never thought of that," said Tammy.

"Let's take a look at your Vegas trips for a second, if you don't mind," said Alan. "A little thought experiment."

"Have at 'er," said Fred.

"You said you go about six times a year?"

"That's right."

"And make five grand each, every trip?"

"Yeah."

"OK. So ten grand between the two of you, six times a year. That's $60,000 annually. And you've been doing this for twenty years?"

Tammy nodded, smiling to herself, realizing what was coming.

"That's $1.2 million," said Alan. "Suddenly, gifting your three sons three hundred grand each doesn't seem so daunting, now does it?"

Fred and Tammy glanced at one another, smiles on their faces.

"I guess all that talk of us being expert accountants is seeming like a lot of bluster at this point," said Fred.

The table laughed.

"Like I said, it's the endowment effect," said Alan. "It goes to a different part of the brain. We don't even think about it. It's only when you look back over a long period of time that you start to see the cumulative effect of what could've been saved. Because a dollar is a dollar no matter how you slice it."

"Still, though," said Rusty, looking at Fred, "it's a hell of a watch."

The group all laughed.

"Maybe we'll skip the Chanel store on our next trip," said Tammy.

"I just can't believe we didn't put this together ourselves," said Fred. "I feel a little embarrassed."

"Not at all," said Alan. "It happens to everyone. And besides—you've given *me* a gift."

The Thurmans looked at him.

"You've given me the perfect example for why even accountants need financial advisors."

Chapter 11
TRANSITIONS

A LARGE PROCESSION of fishermen marched up Fort Square carrying an enormous seven-hundred-pound statue of St. Peter on their shoulders. The narrow road was adorned with colorful banners and Italian flags and scores of jubilant spectators all tossing flowers, lighting candles, some intoning prayers to that patron saint of fishermen and to the brave fishermen themselves who walked so proudly dressed in their pristine white button-ups, white trousers, and white shoes.

It was the last day of Novena, a nine-day period of prayer, culminating in the opening of St. Peter's Fiesta to begin the following morning, and from the Beauport Hotel patio, the league all regarded the procession passing by as they lunched. As the fishermen headed up to Commercial Street, continuing the annual tradition that had been started by the city's Sicilian descendants nearly a hundred years ago, there could be heard half a dozen celebratory church bells ringing out in the distance and the sounds of the carnival being set up in St. Peter's Square beyond. A large Ferris wheel already towered over the waterfront, the pleasant smell of fresh popcorn and funnel cakes on the breeze.

Yet dominating the senses of the group was, as always, that week's repast. A silky lobster carbonara with tender chunks of meat and crispy guanciale and buttery spaghetti al dente, all served in a creamy sauce made from egg yolks, cream, and Parmigiano-Reggiano cheese. This week was to be the league's final lunch, the last of their long and fruitful sessions, and every member seemed to be savoring each and every bite of their meal with greater relish, each mouthful of their dessert sorbet, each sip of their espresso. Like the last day of high school, it was a somewhat bittersweet congregation, with the group both looking forward to what lay ahead and yet sad to have the sessions come to an end.

"So what's in the bags?" said Rusty, smirking before taking a sip of his coffee.

Alan looked at him and then glanced at the table beside him, where fourteen small gift bags were all in a row. He looked back at Rusty with a smile and then turned to the rest of the group.

"These last several weeks, I've been fortunate enough to have you all share your stories with me," he said. "And now, if you'll indulge me, I'd like to share a story with you."

He turned back to Rusty.

"And *then* we'll discuss the party favors."

Rusty laughed. "Hey, it's your show, Skip."

"Well, with the St. Peter's Fiesta starting up tomorrow, seeing the fishermen march by," said Alan, "I'm reminded of an old client of mine. A friend, actually. He's a fisherman himself, not by trade, but it's something he's gotten into in his retirement. He's settled down in Key West, and he just loves it. The deep-sea, big-game kind of fishing. Marlin, swordfish, king mackerel. He's always been a great admirer of Hemingway's, so I've no doubt that colored his decision. Though I was happy to see he'd decided to spend his time out on the water and not warming a barstool in sloppy joes."

The group laughed.

"And the reason I bring him up is that I want to talk about transitions," continued Alan. "About the key turning points in our lives that, if we're not careful, can be greatly affected by the various biases we've been discussing these last several weeks. Because when we go through major life transitions—be it retirement, divorce, kids, selling your business, maybe a major health crisis—we're naturally under a lot of stress and so multiple biases often kick in at once, and if you don't handle them right, you'll survive perhaps, but you definitely won't thrive. And if you handle them *really* poorly, then things can go completely to pieces. I often wonder if people's mid-life crises are triggered by this. And so, with the hopes of his example rubbing off on all of us, I want to tell you about my friend Gerry, who, in my opinion, has navigated his own life transitions with grace, aplomb, and good humor.

"You see, about ten years ago—Gerry's in his early seventies now, so we're talking early sixties—he was starting to turn his mind toward retiring. He's an extremely successful guy, a rock star in the medical sales world, and in just about every niche . . . pharmaceuticals, medical devices, biotech. He just knows how to talk to people. One of those guys who could make you feel in ten minutes like you'd known him for ten years. Well, so in his early sixties, he decides it's time to retire. He'd more than enough wealth to live comfortably for the rest of his life, he'd achieved all his career goals, and he wanted to spend more time with kids and his young grandkids.

"But he quickly found out that retiring was much easier said than done. I mean, he just couldn't see himself doing anything else. He'd worked ever since he was very young. So winding down his professional activities seemed impossible to him. He just couldn't imagine getting out of the business. It's who he was. It was his identity, and it's what he enjoyed. And I see this a lot when I talk to people who've worked their whole lives, especially if it's in the same profession. All of a sudden, they get close to retiring, and it just becomes extremely stressful. They don't know what to do. They didn't realize just how much of their identity was tied up in their career. When you go from Dr. Jones to just *Gerry*, it can be very jarring. You're no longer the most important person in the room, and you just feel like you've fallen off the face of the earth. You've no idea who you are anymore. And whether you're a doctor or a business owner or whatever it is, if your identity is rooted in one thing and that thing goes away, then you're in big trouble."

"So what'd he do?" said Natalie.

"Well, the first thing he did was start talking about it," said Alan. "He and I were close, and so we'd have long conversations discussing what he might do. He *wanted* to retire, to put it behind him and spend more time with his family, but he just couldn't. But talking about it was the first step, because it led to him, at least, becoming aware of the problem, and obviously you can't fix something until you know it's broken. And after that, he started preparing. He pushed his retirement date by two years and then actively, step by step, started to implement changes that would gradually make his transition into retirement as smooth as possible."

"Like what kind of changes?" said Ed. "Some of us here are nearing retirement age, so a few pointers might not be a bad idea."

Alan smiled. "Well, he started by taking half days on Friday and then eventually started taking Fridays off completely. He also began slowly delegating some of his responsibility to his co-workers. He started to mentor some of the staff and soon began feeling that the company was in good hands as he'd vetted the next generation of sales reps himself. Things like that. Once he realized what the problem was, and that there was nothing he could do to stop it—I mean, age gets us all sooner or later, right?"

"Speak for yourself," joked Susan.

Alan laughed. "Well, then he found it a little easier to deal with. He started spending more time with his grandkids, exploring new hobbies, took up fishing. He'd always fantasized about moving to Key West, had talked about doing it his entire life, and now he had the perfect excuse to do so.

"And seeing this—seeing my friend go through this change—it was a great windfall for me as well because it showed me that awareness leads to preparedness and preparedness can get you through just about anything. It can make you thrive and not just survive. But unfortunately, most people don't prepare for these major transitions in their lives. What most people do is they instead say to themselves, *OK, I'm working right now, and when it's time to retire, my instincts will take over, and that will take care of that.* But of course, as you have all so colorfully demonstrated over the last several weeks, allowing your instincts to take over isn't always the best decision. It's how biases form, whether it's recency bias or narrative bias or whatever. Because biases can only flourish when we're complacent, and inertia is a powerful force. But awareness, preparedness—these are the opposite of complacency and, thus, why they're so important when navigating important, potentially life-altering moments in your life. When going through transitions."

Alan took a sip of his espresso before continuing.

"That was another windfall for me, stumbling across this concept of transitions," he said. "It's something Gerry and I've discussed a lot. Because transitions can be incredibly daunting. But by viewing them *as* transitions and not the complete end of something, the destruction of your identity or what-have-you, you can handle them much more efficiently and make sure you don't get stuck in certain traps. Like being unable to pull the trigger on retirement and still working into your seventies and eighties. And so Gerry and I began to reflect on other transitional periods in his life.

"For example, Gerry and his wife initially had trouble starting a family together. And this would take them through a multitude of transitions in and of itself. Going through the difficulty of unsuccessfully trying to have children was a transition. Then accepting that it wasn't going to happen was a transition. Deciding to adopt and then going through that whole process was a transition. And then they actually had two adopted kids to look after. Twin baby boys."

"Oh, how adorable," said Tracy.

"And that took some getting used to," said Alan. "But things got even more interesting when Gerry's wife found out she was pregnant."

"Oh my goodness," said Natalie. "They had *three* kids all at once?"

Alan shook his head. "Not three," he said.

"You're kidding," said Susan.

"Four," said Alan. "His wife was pregnant with twins herself."

The entire table gasped with surprise and thrill.

"*Two* sets of twins?" said Natalie.

"Uh-huh," said Alan. "Four baby boys. The pairs just eight months apart."

"Now *that's* a transition," said Rusty.

The group all laughed.

"And how'd they make out?" said Mark.

"Fantastic," said Alan. "I've met their boys, and they've all grown up to be very polite, very successful men. But needless to say, it was definitely a learning curve."

"No kidding," said Natalie. "One baby's hard enough, but *four*? Sheesh."

"Well, actually, Gerry has six kids. Two from his first marriage. A marriage that was, well . . ."

"A transition?" said Mark with a smile.

"That's putting it lightly," said Alan. "And a poorly navigated one on Gerry's part. By his own admission. I mean, it was a rough partnership from the get-go. They really never should've gotten married to begin with. But Gerry, looking back on it now, realized that he just couldn't bring himself to call it off at the time. Couldn't bear to go through *that* transition. So they had children, which didn't help in terms of relieving their marital stress. But Gerry told himself he'd wait to confront the issue until the kids had grown just a little bit older. Well, that time came and went, and he was still miserable. But inertia can keep a person locked in, can't it?"

"Marriages are tough," said Phil, staring down into his coffee. "Even the good ones."

"Absolutely," said Alan. "And every marriage goes through numerous transitory periods. You've got the fun, romantic, courting stage. The honeymoon stage. Then you've got a kind of partnership, running the 'business' of being married, making financial decisions, and general life decisions together. And then you've got the mature phase. And moving through all those transitions can be very tough. Good marriages can fail because couples don't know how to navigate the transitions, and bad marriages can persist because couples are afraid to transition at all."

"So how's Gerry doing these days?" said Natalie. "Have you seen much of him since he moved down to Key West?"

"Actually, Gerry only moved down there a couple months ago. Only retired last year."

The league all stared back at Alan with surprise on their faces.

"Like I said, transitions can be tough. Though Gerry was working through his issues, aware and prepared, it was still very difficult for him to make that final leap of faith."

"What made him finally jump?" said Mark.

"Well. In a word? Cancer."

A hush sounded around the table.

"It's all right," said Alan. "He was one of the lucky ones. They caught it early, the treatments were successful, and he's been cancer-free for eighteen months now."

"Thank God," said Susan.

"But as he put it himself, it scared him straight. It was a lightbulb moment. It made him step back and say, *Why am I still on this hamster wheel?* And once he got through *that* transition, retirement was a no-brainer. He's said he hasn't looked back since. Because he finally saw himself differently. Not just as some successful salesman, but as a husband and a father and a grandfather. A friend. And just like that, his identity crisis faded into the background. But that's how overwhelming transitions can be. It took him being diagnosed with cancer to step off the train."

"And he's enjoying his retirement?" asked Rusty.

"He's doing great," said Alan. "Loving it down in Key West. He's helped all six of his children get their own careers off the ground, providing them support where they need it, whether financial or otherwise. He and his wife have a very active social life down in Florida, and he's back here in Massachusetts regularly to see his grandkids. I saw him a few weeks ago, actually, and he's just giggly happy with how his life's going ever since he retired. So he's really a case of somebody who did it the right way. Someone who learned from his mistakes and changed his behavior for the better. Someone who now embraces transitions.

"Because transitions are about pivoting to something else, something new and exciting, not about something ending. Most people subconsciously think about retiring as an end, that everything's over, that next I'm going to be pushed out to sea on an ice floe. But the reality is that you've got all this potential freedom and all the finances to do everything that you've ever wanted. But we get used to acting in a certain way, and our brains and our bodies just want to keep on continuing in that way.

"The expression that I often come back to is that everybody wants progress, but nobody wants change. Everybody wants improvement, but nobody wants struggle. But the thing is that progress and improvement *are* change. So we're protecting ourselves from living our best lives because, as they say, when we get into a rut, we like to decorate it. But to me, the absolute saddest thing in life is either to skip a stage or refuse to move onto the next one. But I hope that what you've all learned here these last few weeks will help you move through each stage, each transition, with a better understanding of not just the whys behind your financial decisions, but also behind your broader life decisions. Now then . . ."

Alan rose in his seat, went to the table all stacked with gift bags, and began collecting several at a time, handing them out to the league.

"To thank you for some of the most rewarding conversations I've had in my life, I've gone ahead and got you all a little something," he said.

When the group had all received their gifts, they glanced around the table with expectant expressions on their faces before turning back to Alan. He stared back with a smile and an eyebrow raised in a gesture that they go ahead. The league smiled back, anxious with anticipation, before looking around the table once more.

Then they opened the bags.

Chapter 12

RATIONAL FINANCE

NSIDE EACH gift bag was a small box of gourmet chocolate truffles, a sealed baronial envelope, and a large leather-bound journal embossed with a stylized image of a lobster on the front. The group all glanced around at one another with touched expressions on their faces before looking back at Alan. He sat once more, took another sip of coffee, and then looked around the table.

"My mother used to give me a box of those same truffles at the end of any big milestone," he said. "Graduation, my twenty-first birthday, when we New Hampshire Wildcats won the NCAA Division I Ice Hockey Championship."

"Go 'Cats," said Rusty.

Alan smiled. "She got the idea from a patient of hers," he said. "She was a nurse at Mass General, worked in outpatient oncology, and she told me that this patient of hers received those same truffles from her children after completing a very difficult round of chemotherapy. Well, the patient decided to give the truffles to my mother, saying she couldn't have gotten through the treatments without her graceful bedside manner. Beyond that, she only told her to pay it forward. And she passed that lesson on to me as well.

"The reason I created the Lobster League, why we've gathered here at the Beauport every Tuesday for the last several weeks," he continued, "was to discuss financial and critical life decisions—those that worked and those that didn't—in order to illuminate the various biases, the mental shortcuts, that can potentially lead us down a bad path. And what I want to leave you with today, what I *really* want to pay forward, is the antidote to the bad medicine of biases. What I call *Rational Finance*.

"So what is Rational Finance? Well, for starters, it's the opposite of making biased decisions. It's making decisions that are not governed by emotions, but by logic and reason, that allow us to conduct ourselves in a more measured manner. Commonplace financial theory assumes that investors *already* make rational decisions, but as we've proven, this is certainly not always the case. Behavioral theory, on the other hand, explains the precise reasons why people, in fact, do *not* act rationally, and Rational Finance explains how people can correct this and make logical, beneficial choices when it comes to their wealth.

"OK. So, how do people actually do that? How do we take advantage of all we've learned about how biases work? First, we need to understand that the brain is always going to take shortcuts. Always. It's just how we're programmed. And being part of the Lobster League, I hope, has proven that to be true for all of you."

"It certainly has," said Phil.

"And why exactly is that?" said Natalie. "We're all intelligent people, so how come it's only now, at these lunches, that we've become cognizant of patterns that, in hindsight, seem to be fairly obvious?"

"Because you've been experiencing those patterns through third parties," said Alan. "We all know we have blind spots, and we all know that even if someone points out these blind spots to us, we can sometimes fail to see them. Whether out of ego or shame or whatever it might be. But when we're listening to a third party tell their own story, inadvertently revealing their own blind spots to us, then we start to see the same behavior in ourselves. We're not being judged or appraised. We're just listening and realizing that the person across the table from us is human, makes human mistakes, and that we make those same mistakes too. Hearing someone else discuss their thoughts often clarifies our own thoughts, doesn't it?"

The table all nodded in agreement.

"I mean, personally, after studying this stuff for over twenty years, I *still* have a problem with recognizing my own patterns," said Alan. "I still laugh at how many times I get sucked into behavioral biases. But what I've learned to do is to back up and say, OK, now that you recognize the way that the brain works, what are the next steps that need to happen?"

Ed smiled. "And?"

"And the next step is to be clear about what you want," said Alan. "And how do you clarify to yourself what it is that you want? You write it down. Which is why I've gifted you the journals."

"They're beautiful," said Jane, opening hers up and admiring the shimmering blank pages.

"When you write down what you want, it becomes clear to you. It becomes more than just an abstract thought. And what I tell people is to write down as many things as possible—ten things, a hundred things, the more the merrier—because then you can compare the listed wants with each other and see what it is you truly want most. So writing down what you want and then prioritizing the list is the first step in my Rational Finance framework."

"You mean writing down what we want in terms of *finances*?" said Gina.

"No," said Alan. "I mean what you want out of life. Your goals, your dreams. Because that's what the wealth is for, after all, isn't it? And armed with your list, you can then begin to think about making a decision. You can begin to think, *OK, this is important, but where does it stand in terms of priority*? And thereafter, you can start to make sure that the order is correct and that it continues to be correct as things in your life change. As you move through transitions.

"We cannot help biases from emerging. So don't bother fighting them. Just understand that the brain is an amazing system and the number of decisions that it has to process on a daily basis is astronomically vast. I mean, they say we make around thirty-five thousand decisions per day, and about ninety-five percent of those are subconscious. So just accept the fact that that's how we work. But at the end of the day, what Rational Finance teaches us is that each individual conscious decision that you make should be defined in two ways: Is it helping me live the most satisfying life, or is it not? That's what the prioritized list is for. And by paying attention to that, by actively thinking about what's most important to you in your life, you can start moving toward the most satisfying life possible."

"Thirty-five thousand decisions *per day*?" said Marjorie.

"Sheesh," said Rusty. "I can barely decide between soup or salad."

The table all laughed.

"You see now why biases are so common," said Alan. "Our decisions are constantly shaped by the brain's natural tendency to simplify information through heuristics. These mental shortcuts are essential—they allow us to make the countless decisions required each day just to survive. Even basic functions like breathing or simple movements rely on these automatic processes. More complex tasks, such as driving a car, involve so many calculations and actions that the brain must rely on shortcuts to manage them efficiently. If you observe any animal, you'll notice they perform remarkably complex actions and make split-second decisions, and all without the 'rational' part of the brain that humans possess. We share this instinctive brain—our 'lizard brains'—with other animals, but what sets us apart is our rational, conscious mind. This part of our brain enables us to experience deep emotions and achieve extraordinary things, like sending people to the moon.

"However, our brains evolved over millions of years, long before we had to face modern challenges like making complex financial decisions. These types of decisions are so new in evolutionary terms that our brains weren't built for them. That's where the Lobster League comes in. It was designed to help us all recognize how these mental shortcuts can influence decision-making—often without us realizing it—by exploring our real-world examples. As we become more aware of how these unconscious forces shape our choices, we can better accept that they're simply part of how our brains work. There's no escaping them—but there is learning how to manage them.

"As a financial advisor with over thirty years of experience, helping clients understand and overcome these unconscious influences is hands-down the greatest challenge that I face. But it's the key to helping people make thoughtful, purposeful decisions that lead to a fulfilling life. A life without regret.

"So be very clear about what you want. And to be clear, write it down. Write and then prioritize what you've written. Then, start laying out very clear steps that will help you achieve those goals, which include making sure that your tools and investment decisions match those goals. This, of course, is more complex than it sounds and requires not only understanding clearly what you want to accomplish but also the intricate differences of types of investments, insurance, real estate, tax, and other parts of managing personal finance."

"But if you don't start somewhere, you'll never start at all," said Phil.

Alan smiled. "Exactly. And once we have that sorted, then we test and retest, continually verifying that what we have set out to accomplish is still important to you. This helps when we reach a transition stage like retirement, divorce, the birth of children or grandchildren. Anything, really. And by following this framework, we create a more complex decision-making process that helps to limit the effects of the brain simplifying things. Without following a framework, people instead make decisions that 'feel good,' which results in a big misalignment between what people describe as a satisfying life and a wealthy life. And from my experience, this misalignment is found in over 90 percent of people."

Alan took another sip of his coffee and then took a moment before readdressing the group. A look of tender contemplation crossed his face.

"The purpose of these meetings," he said, "was to make it as simple and impactful as possible for you all to better understand biases and then to provide a concise framework with which to guard against such biases in the future. At the end of the day, the number of choices that people make regarding how to both spend and invest their money is just so vast that we lose sight of how each single investment decision shapes our lives. And I want to move each of you closer to your most satisfying life.

"*That's* what I'm here for," Alan said with a smile. "I'm an expert in many different areas of investment, and by understanding what people want to accomplish, by understanding the full picture of their finances, it's easier to be able to help them make investment choices as opposed to making investment choices and then figuring out how they're going to fit their lives into those decisions. What I do is advise people. And my advice is solely based on helping others achieve what they want. To achieve their purpose. Nothing more, nothing less."

He cleared his throat. A swell of emotion rising within him.

"And so in closing, I just wanted to say to you all—thank you for joining me these last weeks, for your candor and your kindness, and for allowing me to continue achieving *my* purpose. For allowing me to pay it forward."

The league all thanked him in kind, some so touched they dabbed tears from their eyes, others looking on with stoic resignation.

"I gotta ask," said Rusty, looking at Alan.

The group all turned to him, and Rusty held up the baronial envelope that had been included in his and everyone else's gift bag.

"What's behind door number three?"

Alan laughed. "A call to action," he said. "For those of you curious about learning more."

Then, with nothing else, Alan rose in his seat, and everyone else followed suit, and it was a long few minutes as they all hugged one another and offered heartfelt goodbyes. There were warm remarks and teary sentiments and promises to stay in touch, and they soon all turned and looked out over the water. An old seine boat was being walked down the beach by a twelve-person crew, all laughing in revelry as they launched the vessel, a final rehearsal before the official boat races of the St. Peter's Fiesta commenced that coming weekend. The league watched them begin to depart into the water, the smells of the carnival midway on the breeze, the wild calls of oystercatchers sounding out over the harbor, and as they watched that crew of a dozen-strong work together, navigating their boat out into the water amidst the shining midday sun, it was not lost on them that they too were all now headed toward some bright shimmering tomorrow.

"To fair winds, full nets, and safe returns," said Alan, smiling to himself, still staring out over the harbor.

"To the Lobster League," said Rusty.

The others all smiled and, still looking out over the water themselves, each and every one of them began to intone under their breath that selfsame toast, that simple yet stirring hail to both their group and to that indefinable collective spirit they'd encountered weekly those last powerful months.

To the Lobster League.

NOTE FROM THE AUTHOR

DEAR READER,

Thank you for taking a chance on my book. As a financial advisor, it has long been my goal to share my experience with a wider audience so that more people can make confident, well-informed financial decisions.

One area where I see people struggle most is in choosing the right advisor. Too often, investors end up with someone they simply like or happen to know socially. While relationships matter, the real test of an advisor is whether they can guide you through tough decisions and complex questions. This is especially true when things don't go as planned, as inevitably, they do.

When evaluating an advisor, here are four essential questions to ask:

1. Are we a good fit?

This goes beyond personality or social circles. A true advisor should be willing to challenge you, provide perspective during difficult times, and help you make hard choices—not just nod along.

2. What do you offer?

Look for a fee-only advisor who acts as a fiduciary—meaning they are obligated to put your best interests first. They should not sell products or earn commissions. If you receive a vague or complicated answer here, ask for it in writing. A trustworthy advisor should have nothing to hide.

3. What is your process for getting started?

A sound process begins with listening—understanding who you are, your current situation, and what you want to achieve. Beware of anyone eager to rush you into decisions without first taking the time to understand your goals. It's like calling an electrician for backyard lighting and being told, without any discussion, you need a new furnace—solutions without context rarely serve your needs.

4. What is your experience?

This may seem obvious, but many people calling themselves "comprehensive advisors" are actually salespeople or relationship managers with little direct experience providing financial advice. The person you work with should have the background, training, and judgment to guide you effectively.

If you keep these questions in mind, you'll be far more likely to find an advisor who is not only capable but truly aligned with your best interests.

Above all, I hope this book has helped you recognize the role that knowledge, discipline, and awareness of our own biases play in making sound financial choices. Thank you again for reading—and here's to your financial clarity and success.

Yours sincerely,

Scott R. MacKenzie, MBA, CFP®, CIMA®, CLU®
PFW Advisors